Healing in the Catholic Church

Healing in the Catholic Church:

mending wounded hearts and bodies

Rev. Joseph Champlin

OUR SUNDAY VISITOR, INC.
HUNTINGTON, INDIANA 46750

Nihil Obstat:
Rev. David W. Barry
Censor Librorum

Imprimatur:
✝ Frank J. Harrison, D.D.
Bishop of Syracuse
November 1, 1984

The *Nihil Obstat* and *Imprimatur* are official declarations that a book or pamphlet is free of doctrinal or moral error. No implication is contained therein that those who have granted the *Nihil Obstat* and *Imprimatur* agree with the contents, opinions, or statements expressed.

ISBN: 0-87973-719-0
LCCCN: 84-62226

Cover design by
James E. McIlrath

Published, printed, and bound in the U.S.A. by
Our Sunday Visitor, Inc.
200 Noll Plaza
Huntington, Indiana 46750

719

ACKNOWLEDGMENTS

The author and publisher are grateful to the authors, publishers, and others cited in the chapter notes at the end of this book for the use of material excerpted from their works appearing throughout this book. Special thanks go to the following: Confraternity of Christian Doctrine for the use of Scripture taken from the *New American Bible*, © 1970 by the Confraternity of Christian Doctrine, Washington, D.C.; all rights reserved. International Committee on English in the Liturgy, Inc. (ICEL), for excerpts from the English translation of the *Rite of Funerals*, © 1970, ICEL; excerpts from the English translation of *The Revised Order of Blessing an Abbot or Abbess, of Consecration to a Life of Virginity, and of the Blessing of Oils*, © 1971, ICEL; excerpts from the English translation of *Pastoral Care of the Sick: Rites of Anointing and Viaticum*, © 1984, ICEL; all rights reserved. Paulist Press for material reprinted from *Praying for Inner Healing*, by Robert Faricy, S.J., © 1979 by Robert Faricy; used by permission of the Paulist Press. St. Anthony Messenger Press for a selection taken from *Learning to Live Again: The Journey Through Grief for the Widowed or Divorced*, by Judith Tate, © 1979 by St. Anthony Messenger Press, 1615 Republic St., Cincinnati, OH 45210; all rights reserved. Ave Maria Press for excerpts from *The Prayer That Heals*, by Francis MacNutt, © 1981; *To Heal As Jesus Healed*, by Barbara Leahy Shlemon, Dennis Linn, and Matthew Linn, © 1978; and *The Healing Power of the Sacraments*, by Jim McManus, © 1984; used by permission of Ave Maria Press, Notre Dame, IN 46556; all rights reserved. The *National Catholic Register* for "The Gift of Healing," by Charlotte Hayes (March 4, 1984 edition); reprinted by permission of the *National Catholic Register*. The *New Covenant* for material from the article "In the Name of Jesus, Run!" by Myles Maynard (July/August 1984 edition), *New Covenant*, P.O. Box 7009, Ann Arbor, MI 48107; reprinted with permission. *Harper's* for an excerpt from "Making Medical Mistakes," by David Hilfiker, © 1984 by *Harper's Magazine*; all rights reserved; reprinted from the May 1984 issue by special permission. Schocken Books, Inc., for excerpts from *When Bad Things Happen to Good People*, by Harold S. Kushner, © 1982 by Harold S. Kushner; reprinted by permission of Schocken Books, Inc. *The Christian Century*, for excerpts from "Grief and the Art of Consolation: A Personal Testimony," by Troy Organ (August 1-8, 1979 edition), *The Christian Century*, 407 S. Dearborn, Chicago, IL 60605; reprinted with permission. William Morrow and Co., Inc., for excerpts from *The Man Beneath the Gift: The Story of My Life*, by Ralph A. DiOrio with Donald Gropman, © 1980 by Ralph A. DiOrio and Donald Gropman; reprinted by permission of William Morrow and Co., Inc. Harper and Row, Publishers, Inc., for specified excerpts from *Healing and Christianity: In Ancient Thought and Modern Times*, by Morton T. Kelsey, © 1973 by Morton T. Kelsey, and specified excerpts from *A Severe Mercy*, by Sheldon Vanauken, © 1977, 1980 by Sheldon Vanauken, both reprinted by permission of Harper and Row, Publishers, Inc.

Dedicated to
Father Kevin Joseph Murphy
(Born 1950 — Died 1984)
†
Zealous lover of the Church,
sensitive servant
to the young and hurting,
inspiration
throughout months of pain.

Contents

Introduction
11

CHAPTER 1
Holy People and Holy Places
14

CHAPTER 2
Remarkable People in Unusual Locations
23

CHAPTER 3
The Master Healer
34

CHAPTER 4
Ordinary People and Everyday Places
42

CHAPTER 5
Present and Past Obstacles
50

CHAPTER 6
A Long and Continuous Tradition
60

contents —————— continued

CHAPTER 7
Mending Wounded Hearts and Bodies
68

CHAPTER 8
Comforting and Curing the Sick
82

CHAPTER 9
Inner Healing
93

CHAPTER 10
Preparing for the Journey
118

CHAPTER 11
Comfort for Those Who Mourn
130

CHAPTER 12
*The Ultimate Healing,
Or Why Bad Things Happen to Good People*
154

Notes
168

Introduction

My first and last encounters with Kevin Murphy occurred in Holy Family Church at Fulton, New York.

The initial meeting happened after I became pastor of that parish and Kevin had begun his studies for the priesthood. During vacation periods we would have an occasional meal together, visit, and talk about his future.

Although he was serious-minded, Kevin had a lively and quick sense of humor. He cherished lofty ideals, yet possessed a practical bent. That combined conscientious and pragmatic character led him over the years during summertimes from waterfront swimming instructor to lifeguard supervisor for the city — a very responsible position.

After four years at the Theological College of Catholic University in Washington, our bishop ordained Kevin to the priesthood. I concelebrated his first Mass with him at Holy Family Church and recall well the sung tribute to Mary he arranged for the liturgy's conclusion.

The newly ordained Father Murphy served as an associate pastor for several years, distinguishing himself, in addition to other ways, by great solicitude for the sick and interest in the young. Eventually Kevin started teaching in a Catholic high school and working in his spare time on diocesan worship events.

Even though liturgy was a great love of his life and he had been appointed executive director of the diocese's liturgical committee, this young man never realized his dreams for our worship renewal. A malignancy changed those plans.

11

Surgery and treatment presumably eliminated the cancerous growth. But Kevin never did regain full strength and endured instead a long, painful episode of operations, treatments, and extended hospitalizations.

Kevin taught and inspired many during these hospital intervals. He would offer Mass in rooms, anoint those seriously ill, and sometimes walk down the corridor carrying an IV bottle as he made his way to comfort a discouraged patient.

His last year on earth was spent continuously in a hospital bed. The excursions of mercy around the building happened less frequent now and finally ceased. But always beside him were the big crucifix and huge rosary beads.

After he died, two nurses entered the room and knelt for ten minutes in prayer by Kevin's bed. He had brought one of the nurses back to the Lord and baptized her three children during a hospital stay. He had instructed and received the other into the Church while hospitalized on another occasion.

I concelebrated his funeral at that same Holy Family Church; a capacity congregation participated in the Mass. We sang at the end, appropriately, a hymn to our Lady. Kevin had often spoken to Christ's Mother these familiar words of the "Ave Maria": "Holy Mary, Mother of God, pray for us sinners now and at the hour of our death." I am sure at the end she responded to Kevin's request, interceded for him, and received him into her arms.

* * *

Kevin Murphy several times asked me to write a book explaining the sacrament of the anointing of the sick. He believed that we were still not fully tapping the riches of this rite. However, it was only after his death that Mr. Robert Lockwood of Our Sunday Visitor, Inc., contacted me about the possibility of undertaking such a project. I am thus especially grateful to him for giving me the opportunity and impetus to fulfill, albeit belatedly, Kevin's wish.

I would like also to extend my appreciation to Father Robert Chryst, Monsignor Robert Davern, Father Neal Quartier, and Mrs. Ann Tully for their willingness to read the manuscript and offer suggestions. J. Murray Elwood introduced me some years ago to Sheldon Vanauken's touching book, *A Severe Mercy* — of which I have included an excerpt in the final chapter of this text. I thank him for that introduction. Finally, my gratitude goes to Mrs. Pat Gale for her usual speedy, accurate typing as well as for her creative research in locating an important resource for me.

Above all, however, I am indebted to the many people whose stories of hurts and healings appear here and make up such an essential part of this book. In nearly all cases their identities have been concealed by a change in name, location, or circumstances. I pray that those lives and these pages will provide hope, courage, and comfort for many who suffer from the wounds which accompany everyone in this life on earth. May they also lead both the writer and his readers to the everlasting world beyond this one.

1

Holy People
and Holy Places

In 1870, a frail but prayerful young man of twenty-five entered the Congregation of Holy Cross in Montreal as a candidate for its brotherhood. Raised almost like an orphan, Alfred Bessette — a simple person with little formal education but rather wise and devout — had attracted the attention and received the support of his pastor in this venture. The priest wrote to the superiors of that community and quite directly told them, "I am sending you a saint."

After the customary period of probation, during which serious doubts arose about Alfred's suitability as a future religious brother because of his fragile health, the Holy Cross Congregation accepted him — although rather reluctantly. They assigned Brother André to a humble post as porter at Notre Dame College in that Canadian city, a position he continued to hold for nearly a half century.

About five years after his religious profession, the self-effacing brother's faith-filled and caring concern for the sick began to produce remarkable effects.

One day, he visited a boy in bed at the infirmary who was afflicted with a severe fever.

"Get up, you lazy fellow," he ordered. "You are in perfect health. Go outside and play."

The young man objected at first but then, feeling much better, got out of bed and went out into the recreation yard. College authorities immediately summoned Brother André and remonstrated with him.

"You had no right to interfere," they complained; "that boy is ill."

"Please permit a doctor to examine him," Brother André replied. "You'll see that St. Joseph cured him."

The doctor came and, after a careful examination of the youth, pronounced him perfectly well.

Shortly thereafter a smallpox epidemic broke out at a nearby college. It struck both students and religious, with some dying as a result of the disease. Brother André volunteered to nurse the ailing there and, upon arrival, knelt and prayed to St. Joseph to protect the sick. No one died after that.

That same year, a colleague named Brother Alderic, bursar at Notre Dame College, was suffering from a serious leg wound which had failed to heal after two months of treatment. Brother André often used some oil from a lamp next to a statue of St. Joseph in his visitations to the sick and had mentioned its wonderful effects to the incapacitated confrere.

The bursar secured a vial of the oil, applied a few drops to his leg wound, prayed to St. Joseph for a cure, and promised that if the saint answered his prayer, he would receive communion the next day in thanksgiving.

The morning after application of the oil, Brother Alderic commented, "I felt no pain. At the end of two days, the wound had completely healed."

Those three occasions when cures were effected through his intercession were the beginning of an immense, unique ministry of healing by the holy Brother André. In 1916 alone, for example, four hundred thirty-five cures were recorded at the shrine dedicated to St. Joseph in Montreal.

15

The community's fears about André's fragile health proved unfounded. André died in 1937 at ninety-one, continuing his life of prayer and healing to the very end.

In June of 1978 — not many years later by Church standards — Pope Paul VI declared Brother André to be "Venerable," the first step toward canonization, and noted how he had practiced the theological and cardinal virtues to a heroic degree.[1]

Pope John Paul II then elevated the humble man a notch higher and on May 23, 1982, named him Blessed André Besette.

* * *

Ordained in 1956, I accepted the possibility of miracles both during the decades before and after I became a priest. But until a few years ago, I judged that miraculous cures, like the ones cited above, happened only in certain holy places and only through connection with certain holy people either still living or now deceased.

My travels have taken me to many of those traditional shrines where cures occur, favors are granted, and petitions seem answered. I celebrated Mass amid the severe beauty of Fatima, immersed myself in the baths at Lourdes, asked St. Francis' help while visiting Assisi, prayed to our Lady in the Miraculous Medal Chapel at the Daughters of Charity motherhouse along Rue de Bac in Paris, spent time at St. Anne's in Quebec, walked the stations of the cross along the ravine in Auriesville at the North American Martyrs Shrine, and — as preparation for this book — made a special trip to Montreal for several hours of prayer, reflection, and study at St. Joseph's Basilica.

In all these spots, however, some holy individual, usually canonized, serves as the sort of conduit for our pleas; among them, for example, are our Lady, St. Joseph, St. Anne, St. Bernadette, St. Francis, St. Vincent, or St. Louise de Marillac. Moreover, those who visited

Mount Royal before Brother André's death considered him to be an exceptionally saintly man, and the young children on whom the vision at Fatima centered were judged uniquely touched by God.

The life of Brother André and the wonders at St. Joseph's Oratory in Montreal exemplify that limited understanding of miraculous healings I possessed from the 1930s until the 1970s.

On my visit to the shrine, I arrived by cab around 6:30 on a cold, damp, and miserable winter morning. A cover of snow concealed the beauty of the finely landscaped grounds, but sight of the massive basilica at a distance rising over five hundred feet above street level left me awed and impressed.

As I entered the grounds proper, I immediately came upon and walked around a large statue of St. Joseph with the Christ Child in his arms and a Latin motto, "*Ite ad Joseph* (Go to Joseph)," chiseled into the base. Those words set the tone for this place of prayer.

There may not be exactly one thousand steps leading to the basilica, but that morning there were certainly more than one thousand votive candles burning in the crypt chapel vestibule. They had been lighted, I mused, by believers urgently expressing requests or fervently giving thanks for petitions already granted.

As I stood in this corridor of candles, I looked up and spotted a vast array of crutches, canes, and braces suspended from the ceiling. Included among them were a pair of children's shoes, a particular poignant testimony to some past cure. All these discarded items, however, were and continue to be silent testimonies to healings attributed during the past century to the prayers of Brother André and the intercession of St. Joseph.

To ease a person's pain or restore an individual's health are desirable efforts and effects in themselves. But the humble doorkeeper looked beyond those immediate, apparent results. God, in Brother André's mind, always wanted healing to produce a deeper spiritual impact — to soften sinners' hearts, to bring the lost back to the Church, to provide courage for those crushed by burdens, to stir up faith in those with little or no belief, to push some to pray better, and to deepen the faith of people already committed to the Lord.

He once remarked, "My greatest pleasure is to reconcile a sinner to God."[2]

The following incident reveals both that desire to facilitate spiritual conversions and his intuitive understanding of a person's inner state. Brother André, besieged by people seeking his help, said to a man approaching him:

"And what can I do for you, sir?"

"My arm is paralyzed; I cannot move it."

"Go to confession and then start a novena."

"I beg your pardon?"

"I said: 'Go to confession and then start a novena.' "

"But I haven't gone to confession for the last twenty-five years."

Vainly the young lady who accompanied the stranger pulled at his arm, saying:

"Be careful, Father, people will hear what you say."

"If I have been bad enough to spend twenty-five years without going to confession, I should be brave enough to admit it."

Brother André interrupted him: "Take your hat with your right hand and put it on."

The man obeyed, not a little stupefied at the surprise of feeling no more pain. Brother André continued:

"Come tonight to sleep in the room under the chapel roof. Tomorrow you will receive Holy Communion."

The recipient of the miracle went away. One of the bystanders said to Brother André:

"You have let him go. Do you think he will come back?"

"Yes, I am sure of it."

The man did come back, went to confession, and received Holy Communion.[3]

Brother André always attributed these marvelous physical and spiritual healings to God but viewed them as achieved through the intercession of St. Joseph. However, he himself often either touched the afflicted with a medal of St. Joseph and rubbed special oil consecrated to that saint upon the ailing spot or told his petitioners to do so.

Dr. Joseph Charette, although a devout Catholic physician, nevertheless frequently criticized Brother André and publicly referred to him as a charlatan, quack, and old fool. He also specifically ridiculed the way the doorkeeper rubbed people with St. Joseph's oil and touched them with a medal, even suggesting that the ascetical brother tainted his vow of chastity in the process.

One day, however, Dr. Charette's wife developed a serious nosebleed and neither he nor several other doctors could stem the hemorrhaging.

"Bring Brother André," the woman demanded of her husband.

"Madame," her husband responded, "I love you very much, but what you ask of me is impossible."

His wife asked insistently:

"Do you wish me, whom you say you love very much, to bleed to death? Get Brother André."

The doctor blanched. What would the neighbors

say if they saw him bringing the "quack" to his home? Love triumphed, however, and the doctor set off with heavy heart to summon the man he had maligned. André met the doctor at the shrine and welcomed him with a smile, saying:

"Doctor, return home; your wife's nosebleed has stopped."[4]

The doctor breathed a sign of relief, for several reasons, at this immediate yet long-distance healing.

Brother André's recourse to the intercession of St. Joseph as well as the faithful's invocation today of Blessed André for assistance rests solidly upon an accepted Catholic teaching and practice.

The communion of saints is a Roman Catholic doctrine that enjoys the support of ancient tradition, is expressed in public worship weekly, has been taught by theologians both past and present, was included in the "Credo of the People of God" proclaimed by Pope Paul VI, and can be found in documents of the Second Vatican Council.

It means a bond, link, or fellowship exists among followers of Christ — that is, members of the Church struggling here on earth, suffering in purgatory, and rejoicing in heaven. These groups — in previous years commonly termed the Church militant, suffering, and triumphant — help one another.

The saints in heaven, according to one well-known modern theologian, "intercede for those of us on earth and place their merits at our disposal."[5]

The Second Vatican Council's "Dogmatic Constitution on the Church" develops at some length this Catholic belief in the communion of saints. It maintains that those holy ones in heaven, like St. Joseph or Blessed Brother André, "do not cease to intercede with the Father for us." It notes how the Church has always believed that these saints "are closely united with us in Christ" and "has asked piously for the help of their intercession." Finally, this document urges as most fitting that we love the saints, give thanks to God for them, and humbly invoke them, requesting their help in "obtaining from God through his Son, Jesus Christ, our Lord, our only Redeemer and Savior, the benefits we need."[6]

Just how our prayers and the intercessions of the saints in heaven bring about those benefits, lead to healings, and accomplish the remarkable results typified by the happenings at the Oratory in Montreal is not so clear, nor are any of the various explanations offered universally endorsed by all theologians. We are in the realm of mystery here, trying to grasp how an eternal, infinite, and unchangeable God deals with temporal, finite, and changeable humans.

St. Thomas Aquinas, the great philosopher and theologian so often quoted in the Church, dedicates an extended section of his famous *Summa Theologica* to questions surrounding intercessory prayer, including this issue of how God responds to our pleas. He asks, "Are the prayers of the saints for us always granted?" St. Thomas first lists objections that they are not, then responds with his own teaching that these petitions are always granted. One reason the Angelic Doctor lists in support of his position struck me: "But in so far as they pray for us by asking something for us in their prayers, their prayers are always granted, since they will only what God wills. . . ."[7]

All seem to agree that our prayers are heard and answered; nevertheless, in what way and why this comes about appear to be puzzles whose solutions elude us here and will remain unsolved until we enter into glory.

Brother André was a holy man who turned Mount Royal into a holy place where healings frequently happened both during his life and after his death. There have been many other such places and persons in the Church's history. But recently we have witnessed a seemingly new and different phenomenon in the United States and abroad. We are seeing people — those with an extraordinary gift for healing — work wonders in the most unusual settings. We will look at that development in the next chapter.

2

Remarkable People in Unusual Locations

Her friends are still skeptical, but Anna E. Hartman of 406 Mersereau Ave., Endicott,* said she really is cured of cancer.

For eight years Hartman suffered from cancer of the neck. She was in and out of hospitals, and was a regular at the cancer clinic at Our Lady of Lourdes Memorial Hospital, 169 Riverside Dr., Binghamton. Since November 1982, however, she has been going less and less frequently, and now only for checkups.

Hartman said she was cured of cancer by Father Ralph A. DiOrio, a healing minister, at a healing Mass in Utica in November 1982.

About 4,000 to 5,000 people attended that day, she said, some who were blind, some in wheelchairs.

"I thought there were people there who needed healing more than I," she said, but DiOrio recognized her pain.

"I went up to the stage, he put his hand around my neck, said a prayer, and I woke up lying on the floor," she said. "I jumped up and haven't had any pain since then."[1]

---

*NOTE: Endicott and the other place-names mentioned in this introduction to Chapter 2 are located in New York state.

* * *

During the past decade or so there have emerged in this country, and I presume elsewhere, numerous women and men who appear to possess unique gifts to heal and who exercise these powers, sometimes in very unusual places.

Father Ralph A. DiOrio, the healer of Anna Hartman, is today perhaps the most notable throughout the United States. But there are many others — people like Brennan, Kelleher, Kuhlman, the Linn brothers, MacAlear, MacNutt, Shlemon, just to name a few — whose words and touch have brought both internal and external cures, physical and spiritual healings, to thousands who have approached them.

These gifted healers often work their wondrous deeds in churches much as Brother André did at the massive St. Joseph's Oratory in Montreal. But they likewise conduct healing services in such unlikely locations as theaters, football stadiums, and exposition grounds. For example, the Mass in Utica, New York — at which Anna Hartman experienced her cancer cure — took place in the War Memorial Auditorium, a civic center capable of handling crowds of more than five thousand.

I would like to describe briefly the work of three contemporary healers — Fathers Edward McDonough, Matthew Swizdor, and Ralph DiOrio — so that through those sketches we can understand a bit better this current phenomenon.

• Redemptorist Father Edward McDonough, ordained in 1948, labored as a parish priest, preached novenas, served the black community of the South, and was pastor of a parish in Roanoke, Virginia, before starting his healing-and-restoration ministry in 1975. Today that apostolate he directs includes a telephone prayer line where people can call for prayers to share their thanksgivings together with a Monday-through-Saturday evening prayer meeting where members ask God's blessing upon their healing ministry and petition the Lord for all who seek their help and prayers.

The mission church or basilica for this ministry at Boston is filled for sessions even though it is located in a rather deteriorated Roxbury section of the city, which might keep interested people from coming at night.

Here is how the Redemptorist priest describes the prayer-healing gatherings he conducts: "This service is a paraliturgical service. It is a prayer service for healing. The purpose of this service is to establish a community of faith and prayer to seek together the healing love of Jesus and His Holy Spirit. We pray for all in the community as well as those we represent, love, and pray for. We pray for spiritual, emotional, and physical healing. In this prayer service all who are praying together form a prayer team to bring God's healing to each individual. The emphasis is on the power of united prayer rather than on receiving an individual prayer blessing."

Does this united community prayer for healing achieve results?

A great-grandmother would give a quick affirmative answer. With great faith she brought her two-year-old great-grandchild to the mission church. Born with the umbilical cord wrapped around her body, not expected to live, and given two months of intensive hospital treatment, the little one was blessed by Father McDonough in 1983. A reexamination afterward indicated there was no longer any damaging brain fluid and, while not completely cured, she can now look forward to a near-normal life.

Joseph McLaughlin would concur with the great-grandmother above. A cancerous tumor on his neck had so advanced that doctors refused to remove it. Friends of Joseph, several motorcycle policemen who voluntarily protect the people and their cars at the church, suggested he go to the healing service. He came for two years and prayed very hard; today, CAT (computerized axial tomographic) scans show his tumor has disappeared. Doctors offer no medical explanation.

Joanne Riccardi likewise believes in the power of this community healing prayer. She came to a Holy Spirit Parish breakfast at the Worcester Marriott Hotel with severe back pains that had burdened her for many years and caused her to schedule a hospital visit. The Redemptorist prayed over her at the breakfast, the pains disappeared, and she canceled the appointment.[2]

• Father Matthew Swizdor conducted a prayer-and-healing service at Sacred Heart Parish in Syracuse during 1983.

One middle-aged woman we will call Mary knew very little about this priest but went to that large church for the evening ceremony so she could pray for two people, a relative and a friend, both dying of cancer. When Father Swizdor invited participants forward for the laying on of hands, Mary did so, and as he touched her she felt stunned, walked back to her place in the pew, and collapsed into a semiconscious state for an hour.

Those regularly involved in this healing ministry would say she was "slain in the Spirit," "falling under the power," or "resting in the Lord." Father Swizdor finds about eighty percent of the people at his services experience a similar phenomenon: they feel a warmth, a lightheadedness, fall down or backward, and become immobilized but remain conscious. He simply explains their reactions in this way: "They are overwhelmed by the power of the Lord."[3]

When Mary got into the car that night to return home, she said to her companion, "I will never smoke again." In fact she has not, even though it meant breaking a forty-year-old habit.

The next evening Mary returned, went forward again, was touched by Father Swizdor, and fell back into the grasp of a waiting usher who assisted her to a seat.

She discovered later that a severe chronic bronchial pain had disappeared.

In some ways this woman had prepared or disposed herself spiritually in advance for such intense and remarkable events. Prior to Father Swizdor's arrival in Syracuse and without any knowledge about him, Mary had started to read the Scriptures regularly. She has continued that practice and now finds herself as well praying a great deal more.

Father Swizdor would not be surprised by this development. He believes that the vast majority of healings are spiritual; that most illnesses stem from frustration, anger, and the abuse of food or drugs; that doctors treat only symptoms while priests and other religious leaders eliminate the core problem which is eating up the inner person; that our generation needs a revival because many have lost faith and are bombarded with materialistic ideas; that healing comes from God; and that faith in the Lord's power normally must be present for a cure to take place.[4]

• Father Ralph DiOrio is the best-known healer of these three. Born in Providence, Rhode Island, in 1930, he studied for the priesthood and was ordained on June 1, 1957 as a member of the Scalabrini congregation, the Missionary Order of St. Charles. After serving in various positions, he asked for and was released from that religious community eleven years later, becoming a secular priest of the Worcester diocese.[5]

His path to the healing ministry began on a Christmas day in 1975 when, discouraged by the poor attendance at morning Mass, he turned to the tabernacle and asked Jesus, the Master, "What else can I do to bring them to a spiritual renewal, to bring them to you?" He felt an inner response, "Ralph, why not try simple, pure me?"

Around that same time he began to experience some

unique feelings within himself. He said: "My body was constantly aflame. When I touched anything, sparks came out of me. Electricity jumped out of my body. I didn't know what was happening. For a while I couldn't touch anything. At first I thought it was a static electric charge from the carpets, but it wasn't, because it happened whether there were carpets or not, and it was stronger than any static charge I had ever felt before. After the electricity started, my knuckles began to hurt, and I thought I was getting arthritis. Then pains began to pass through other parts of my body, and I was frightened because I still didn't know what was happening to me. Now I can see that the Lord, in His Divine Providence, was allowing me to experience the pains of the physical body so I could respond to the pains of others. He was preparing me for my Healing Ministry."

Several months later Father DiOrio visited his seriously ailing mother in Providence. Worried about her condition and angered by his powerlessness to do anything about it, he shouted out in frustration, swore, and banged on the kitchen table. Later, he calmed down and asked his mother's forgiveness. Just as he was about to leave the home and return to his parish, Father DiOrio's mother asked him to pray over her. He once again protested in annoyed frustration but quickly calmed down and reluctantly consented. He tells us: "My mother knelt down, and I laid hands on her head. When she got up, I left. I got in my car and drove back to Fitchburg. When I got there, I phoned my mother. She told me that after I left, she had had a dizzy spell for an hour. And she had felt something go through her body, and she had been healed of her illness. From that moment on, the Spirit was working through me. I still didn't understand or even see what was happening. But I didn't have long to wait."

Father DiOrio's healing gift broke out more openly shortly thereafter at one of Father McDonough's prayer services in Boston. He accompanied some parishioners from Fitchburg who wanted to take part in this charismatic gathering, but he stayed in the rear of the church to avoid being seen by Father McDonough. A small girl of six or seven walked around collecting prayer petitions for the altar and urged DiOrio to write one, suggesting to him that he put down "what is in your heart."

He did so, in Latin, Italian, and Spanish, hoping Father McDonough wouldn't understand his request. Here was the petition which seemed to pour out of him without control: "God, if it be Your Will, give me the fulfillment of my life as a priest. Grant me a new, complete, and worldwide ministry in the Charismatic Renewal, specifically in the Healing Ministry, the thing I have always wanted. Grant me a ministry to heal the bodies and souls of mankind."

Father McDonough eventually spotted him in the shadows and asked him to come forward and preach. Father DiOrio responded with a spontaneous talk on the Blessed Mother which excited the crowd and drew their applause. He then tried to slip away, but . . .

Suddenly a woman ran into the small room where I was and shouted, "Father, hurry up! Quick! My husband is bleeding inside his stomach!"

"Bleeding?" I asked. "Then you have to get him to a doctor. Let's call an ambulance right away and get him to a hospital."

"No! No!" she insisted. "*Pray* over him!"

"Pray over him? Come on," I said, "call the doctor." But this woman would not back down. In fact, she grew even more insistent. "Father!" she demanded. "Pray!"

So I gave in to it. All right, I said to myself, I'll pray. And I did, and poom! The man went down. Just like that. In a minute he looked up at me and said, "I feel great! The pain has gone! My ulcers don't seem to be bleeding anymore!"

My natural instinct was to wonder if the man was pulling my leg. It didn't make any sense. He is bleeding, I pray over him, and all of a sudden the bleeding stops and he's okay? I felt certain he was tricking me for some reason of his own. How slow I was to believe what was happening to me.

Then I wondered if the man was crazy. He didn't look crazy, though. He was just an ordinary-looking, well-dressed middle-aged man, and while I was wondering about him, he got up, brushed himself off and went back to his seat singing, "Hallelujah!"

Thus started Father DiOrio's healing ministry, which swiftly mushroomed and spread around the United States and beyond. On a plane trip to the Midwest recently I sat next to a wealthy woman from Florida who is a strong supporter of the New England priest's work. She spoke of him with great respect and displayed a brochure outlining the man's busy, extensive schedule for the year ahead. He would indeed be leading prayer services and healing events all over this country in both expected places like churches and unusual locations like convention arenas.

But despite the wide popularity, the huge crowds, and the remarkable results, Father DiOrio reminds everyone that the healing is from God alone, that authentic physical healings are accompanied by inner or spiritual healings, that no rivalry does or should exist between healing ministers and the medical profession, and that prayer and fasting remain essential preparatory ingredients for every healing service.

Normally, Father DiOrio experiences an empathic pain as an early indication of a specific healing. He feels this pain in his own body, around the area in which someone is receiving a cure. Myles Maynard — a Bronx, New York, resident — described that phenomenon and how the New England priest healed him of painful, crippling rheumatoid arthritis that had been plaguing him for eleven years.

In 1978 a cousin wrote to the Maynards about Father DiOrio. Even though the husband had just then signed a release for further medication which would require hospitalization because of the side effects, his wife Margaret convinced him to postpone the new treatment and fly with her to Worcester for one of Father DiOrio's services.

Worcester has a small airport, and passengers leave the plane by stairs rather than a ramp. Halfway down I had to stop because of the pain. An attendant rushed up to meet me and asked if he should get a wheelchair. That word "wheelchair" had been haunting me for several years, and I forced myself to make it down the rest of the stairs on my own. When I got to the church I almost had second thoughts because of another long flight of stairs, but with some help I made it.

About an hour into the service I was in considerable pain. Margaret sensed it and later said she had thought I would have to leave. But something seemed to hold me there. Then Father started calling out to those with hearing problems, eye problems, drug problems. He was asking these people to come up to the altar.

At that point a hot feeling started in my feet and traveled up my legs to my shoulders and then down my arms to my fingertips. A religious medal my son-in-law had put around my neck before we left New York became so hot that I had to put my hand inside my shirt and hold the medal away from my skin. At that precise moment Father DiOrio asked the person with arthritis to come up to the altar!

I looked at Margaret, and she was smiling. I went up. Father asked me all about my problem, then asked me to say a prayer with him. He asked if I had felt anything

31

before coming up to the altar, and I mentioned the hot feeling that had gone through my body. He said that had been the Holy Spirit just going through every cell of my body. He prayed over me and said, "He is healed."

Father DiOrio asked how I felt, and I said I had no pain whatsoever. He told me to run to the rear of the church and back again. I explained that I had trouble walking most of the time and did not think I could run. He told me to try it for Jesus, so I trotted to the rear of the church. On my way back he called out, "In the name of Jesus, run!" I began to run, and it felt as though my feet were not even touching the floor. There was no pain at all.

When I got back to the altar Father DiOrio asked Margaret to come up. He asked how long it had been since we had danced together. I told him it had been quite a few years, and he replied, "I want you both to dance to the Anniversary Waltz right here on the altar, so your wife and the congregation can see that you are healed." He turned to the music ministry and instructed them to play the Anniversary Waltz. Well, we are both grown people, but as we danced we cried like babies.

The next morning Margaret and I went to the Worcester airport. Remembering the trouble I had had on the stairs from the plane, I wanted to prove something to myself. I went up those stairs two at a time without any sign of pain.

Our family came over to our place that night and stayed until midnight. I lost count of the times they had me sit down just to see me bounce up like a young kid. My two sons-in-law were getting quite a kick out of shaking hands with me. Before, if someone shook my hand I would almost pass out from the pain.

I had to buy new shoes, because with the swelling

in my feet gone my shoes were all too big. I had to have several links taken out of my watch band because the swelling in my wrist was gone. I was once again able to wear my ring after all those years.

Needless to say, when I got back to work I had to tell the story over and over again. People could not get over the change in me. Quite a few told me their faith had been renewed and strengthened.

There were some skeptics at work who stated that they would hold off their opinions until they heard what my doctor had to say. I kept my regular appointment with him. Usually either the doctor or his nurse would have to help me out of the chair. This time I just popped out of the chair unaided, and I honestly believe the doctor's eyes popped too.

I went through the whole story for him, and then he took blood tests, stress tests, and joint measurements and tested the amount of grip in each hand. He was simply amazed and said my case would probably end up in some medical journal. He told me to cut my medication in half and come back in two weeks. I did not have the heart to tell him I had already stopped medication.

On my next visit I told the doctor I was off medication. He went through all the same tests. His eyes filled up, and he said, "Myles, I have to discharge you because there is nothing wrong with you. We in the medical profession have seen things that have to come from a higher power."[6]

Myles Maynard, healed of his pain, ran in the name of Jesus. Brother André, Father DiOrio, and all the others we have mentioned in between would look upon that same Christ as their model in healing and the ultimate source of their power. As we shall see, Jesus, of course, was — and continues to be — the Divine Physician.

3

The Master Healer

Leprosy, at the time of Jesus, made its victims both hideous to behold and outcasts of society.

It caused the bodily extremities — ears, nose, fingers, toes — to rot away and fall off; it infected the lungs, destroyed the voice box, and brought on blindness; eventually it led to an isolated, painful death.

People in those days avoided lepers, not only because of their ugly wounds and dreadful smells but also because they judged the disease contagious and knew that Jewish law pronounced those so afflicted as legally unclean.

Lepers were forced to remain at a distance, ring a little warning bell as persons approached, and cry out: "Unclean, unclean!"

No wonder that Jesus was "moved with pity" when a leper came forward, knelt down, and asked for a cure (Mark 1:40-41). Moreover, despite the fellow's wretched condition, Christ responded in a caring, surprising, heroic, and powerful manner to the man's plight. He did not flinch and did not run away from the leper. On the contrary, the Great Healer touched this afflicted individual and cured him "then and there" (Mark 1:42).

The Gospel according to Luke, which pictures Jesus so often as the Healer, describes the incident in this way: "On one occasion in a certain town, a man full of leprosy came to him. Seeing Jesus, he bowed down to the ground and said to him, 'Lord, if you will to do so, you can cure me.' Jesus stretched out his hand to touch him and said, 'I do will it. Be cured.' Immediately the leprosy left him. Jesus then instructed the man: 'Tell no one, but go and show yourself to the priest. Offer for your healing what Moses prescribed; that should be a proof for them.' His reputation spread more and more, and great crowds gathered to hear him and to be cured of their maladies. He often retired to deserted places and prayed'' (Luke 5:12-16).

* * *

In addition to preaching the good news of God's love and teaching his listeners how to live, Jesus healed those who came to him with every type of affliction. He brought back to life some who had died, cured countless ones crippled with physical ailments, and freed others from enslaving mental or emotional illnesses.

A few analytical facts about the Gospels' content will indicate just how much of his public ministry Jesus dedicated to healing.[1]

Nearly one fifth of the Gospel texts is given over to Christ's healings and to discussions prompted by these cures. Thus, of the 3,779 verses in the Gospels, 727 specifically treat physical or mental healings and instances of resurrection from the dead. Moreover, 165 verses speak about eternal life, and 31 incidents or references touch upon miracles which include healing.

There are 41 distinct physical and mental healings (72 if you count duplications) recounted in the Gospels plus the innumerable ones covered by general references to a healing of crowds, or multitudes.

While these include a wide variety of both cures themselves and methods of healing, I would like to cite these different kinds, illustrating each with an example.

1. *Cure of a mental or emotional illness.* "In the synagogue there was a man with an unclean spirit, who

35

shrieked in a loud voice: 'Leave us alone! What do you want of us, Jesus of Nazareth? Have you come to destroy us? I know who you are: the Holy One of God.' Jesus said to him sharply, 'Be quiet! Come out of him.' At that, the demon threw him to the ground before everyone's eyes and came out of him without doing him any harm. All were struck with astonishment, and they began saying to one another: 'What is there about his speech? He commands the unclean spirits with authority and power, and they leave.' His renown kept spreading through the surrounding country" (Luke 4:33-37).

2. *Healing of a physical disability, disease, or sickly condition.* "They came to Jericho next, and as he was leaving that place with his disciples and a sizable crowd, there was a blind beggar Bartimaeus ('son of Timaeus') sitting by the roadside. On hearing that it was Jesus of Nazareth, he began to call out, 'Jesus, Son of David, have pity on me!' Many people were scolding him to make him keep quiet, but he shouted all the louder, 'Son of David, have pity on me!' Then Jesus stopped and said, 'Call him over.' So they called the blind man over, telling him as they did so, 'You have nothing to fear from him! Get up! He is calling you!' He threw aside his cloak, jumped up and came to Jesus. Jesus asked him, 'What do you want me to do for you?' 'Rabboni,' the blind man said, 'I want to see.' Jesus said in reply, 'Be on your way! Your faith has healed you.' Immediately he received his sight and started to follow him up the road" (Mark 10:46-52).

3. *Restoration of life to one who had died.* "Soon afterward he went to a town called Naim, and his disciples and a large crowd accompanied him. As he approached the gate of the town a dead man was being carried out, the only son of a widowed mother. A considerable crowd of townsfolk were with her. The Lord was moved with pity upon seeing her and said to her, 'Do

not cry.' Then he stepped forward and touched the litter; at this, the bearers halted. He said, 'Young man, I bid you get up.' The dead man sat up and began to speak. Then Jesus gave him back to his mother. Fear seized them all and they began to praise God. 'A great prophet has risen among us,' they said; and, 'God has visited his people' " (Luke 7:11-16).

We can note in the Gospels, moreover, some half dozen references to occasions where Jesus healed groups of people — uncounted gatherings but classified in terms like a "vast" or "large" crowd.

For example:

"As evening drew on, they brought him many who were possessed. He expelled the spirits by a simple command and cured all who were afflicted, thereby fulfilling what had been said through Isaiah the prophet: 'It was our infirmities he bore, our sufferings he endured' " (Matthew 8:16-17).

"As they were leaving the boat, people immediately recognized him. The crowds scurried about the adjacent area and began to bring in the sick on bedrolls to the place where they heard he was. Wherever he put in an appearance, in villages, in towns, or at crossroads, they laid the sick in the market places and begged him to let them touch just the tassel of his cloak. All who touched him got well" (Mark 6:54-56).

"Coming down the mountain with them, he stopped at a level stretch where there were many of his disciples; a large crowd of people was with them from all Judea and Jerusalem and the coast of Tyre and Sidon, people who came to hear him and be healed of their diseases. Those who were troubled with unclean spirits were cured; indeed, the whole crowd was trying to touch him because power went out from him which cured all" (Luke 6:17-19).

"Later on, Jesus crossed the Sea of Galilee [to the

shore] of Tiberias; a vast crowd kept following him because they saw the signs he was performing for the sick" (John 6:1-2).

At the turn of this century Percy Dearmer in a book entitled *Body and Soul* collected the Gospel healing stories and placed them in an outline on which the entries below, with some modifications, are based. The reader eager to gain a clearer, more complete, and richer picture of Jesus, the Master Healer, from an additional reading of Scripture could find it a helpful reference.[2]

The following consists of instances of *healing*, the *Gospel* (or Gospels) in which they are found, and the *method* involved in bringing about the healing. For example, the first entry indicates the healing of a man possessed by an unclean spirit; reference to this may be found in Mark 1:23 and Luke 4:33; the method employed to heal the individual consists of exorcism through words uttered by Christ.

✓ Man with unclean spirit / Mark 1:23, Luke 4:33 / Exorcism, word.

✓ Peter's mother-in-law / Matthew 8:14, Mark 1:30, Luke 4:38 / Touch, word; friends' prayer.

✓ Multitudes / Matthew 8:16, Mark 1:32, Luke 4:40 / Touch, word; friends' faith.

✓ Many demons / Mark 1:39 / Preaching, exorcism.

✓ A leper / Matthew 8:2, Mark 1:40, Luke 5:12 / Word, touch; leper's faith and Christ's compassion.

✓ A paralytic / Matthew 9:2, Mark 2:3, Luke 5:17 / Word; friends' faith.

✓ Man's withered hand / Matthew 12:9, Mark 3:1, Luke 6:6 / Word; obedient faith.

✓ Multitudes / Matthew 12:16, Mark 3:10 / Exorcism, response to faith.

✓ Jairus's daughter / Matthew 9:18, Mark 5:22, Luke 8:41 / Word, touch; father's faith.

✓ Woman with issue of blood / Matthew 9:20, Mark

5:25, Luke 8:43 / Touching Christ's garment in faith.

✓ A few sick folk / Matthew 13:58, Mark 6:5 / Touch (hindered by unbelief).

✓ Multitudes / Matthew 14:34, Mark 6:55 / Touching Christ's garment, friends' faith.

✓ Woman's daughter / Matthew 15:22, Mark 7:24 / Response to mother's prayer, faith.

✓ Deaf and dumb man / Mark 7:32 / Word, touch; friends' prayer.

✓ Blind man (gradual healing) / Mark 8:22 / Word, touch; friends' prayer.

✓ Child with evil spirit / Matthew 17:14, Mark 9:14, Luke 9:38 / Word, touch; father's faith.

✓ Centurion's servant / Matthew 8:5, Luke 7:2 / Response to master's prayer, faith.

✓ Two blind men / Matthew 9:27 / Word, touch; men's faith.

✓ Dumb demoniac / Matthew 9:32 / Exorcism.

✓ Blind and dumb demoniac / Matthew 12:22, Luke 11:14 / Exorcism.

✓ Multitudes / Matthew 4:23, Luke 6:17 / Teaching, preaching, healing.

✓ Multitudes / Matthew 14:14, Luke 9:11, John 6:2 / Compassion, response to need.

✓ Great multitudes / Matthew 15:30 / Friends' faith.

✓ Widow's son / Luke 7:11 / Word, compassion.

✓ Mary Magdalene and others / Luke 8:2 / Exorcism.

✓ Woman bound by Satan / Luke 13:10 / Word, touch.

✓ Man with dropsy / Luke 14:1 / Touch.

✓ Ten lepers / Luke 17:11 / Word; men's faith.

✓ Servant's ear / Luke 22:49 / Touch.

✓ Nobleman's son / John 4:46 / Word; father's faith.

✓ Man born blind / John 9:1 / Word, touch.

✓ Lazarus / John 11:1 / Word.

It might prove valuable for our discussions later in this book to make a few observations now about the manner in which Christ exercised his healing ministry.

• Jesus cured the sick in various ways, sometimes even at a distance, but his *word* and *touch* most often seemed to be the instruments he employed to heal.

In the illustrations given and the methods described in the listing of Scripture references above, we can see the frequent use of this double approach to healing — a touch from the Master preceded, accompanied, or followed by a word from him. Thus, to further exemplify the point, when two blind men cried out after Jesus, caught up with him, and expressed confidence in his power to heal, the Scriptures tell us: "At that he touched their eyes and said, 'Because of your faith it shall be done to you'; and they recovered their sight" (Matthew 9:29-31).

• Jesus felt deep *compassion* for those suffering in any way.

In a fine jointly authored book on this subject, McNeil, Morrison, and Nouwen observe that the expression "moved with compassion" or "moved with pity" occurs only twelve times in the Gospel and refers exclusively to Jesus or his Father. We saw examples of that phrase above in the incident of the leper and the cure of the widow's son. The Greek word behind this expression captures the intensity of its meaning. Literally we might say that Jesus on these occasions was moved in the entrails, the guts of his body. He felt the pain, anguish, and plight of an afflicted person or crowd of people in the depths of his being. He was profoundly stirred inside which most often led him subsequently to relieve that suffering by some healing deed.[3]

• Jesus somehow appeared *hostile* to whatever force had brought sickness and sufferings to people. This evil power or influence formed an obstacle to Christ's message about freedom and life. Consequently, he rebuked, commanded, and spoke sharply to such a harmful and destructive force.

Morton Kelsey puts it this way: "Jesus seemed to believe that a primary cause of sickness was a force of evil loose in the world which was hostile to God and his way. He believed that men were sometimes in the hands of this power, so that it exerted a baneful influence in their lives. You may call this force Satan, the devil, evil spirits, demons, autonomous complexes, or what you will; its exact source was never fully accounted for. But this understanding, this knowledge of the reality, the fact of such errant destructiveness is shot through the teaching and life of Christ."[4]

• Jesus closely connected *faith and repentance* with his healing deeds. He sometimes demanded both as requisites for a cure; on other occasions, the healing was to bring about belief in him or a conversion of heart for the beneficiary or observers; in every instance, the deeds were to deepen the faith and foster the repentance of all.

In one of his missionary addresses Peter summarized the Master's life: "God anointed him with the Holy Spirit and power. He went about doing good works and healing all who were in the grip of the devil, and God was with him" (Acts 10:38).

However, it appears from sacred Scripture, Church tradition, and contemporary experience that what Jesus did then, he wishes to continue to do in our own day.

4

Ordinary People and Everyday Places

Jane understandably felt deep anxiety when the physician directed her to report without delay for surgery at the hospital. He warned that the lump in her breast was ominous and should be dealt with immediately.

The word cancer and the threat of a malignancy would alarm anyone and certainly a mother of several young children.

She and her husband, Bill, despite their concern about the forthcoming surgery scheduled for Monday, decided to use symphony tickets they had purchased much earlier and attended the Saturday night performance.

During intermission Jane spotted her parish priest in the lobby, went to the man, blurted out her worry, and asked for his prayers. He naturally assured her of them but also summoned the frightened woman's husband over and suggested that the three of them, right then and there in the Civic Center, pray about this situation.

Monday night the priest called their home and inquired about Jane's status. She answered the telephone and gave him this unexpected good news: false alarm, fluid instead of a growth, all clear.

Her surgeon, a Catholic, who had likewise been at the theater on Saturday night, remarked that the prayers must have worked. He fully anticipated discovering an ugly malignant condition and was totally surprised at what he found.

Did Jane experience anything unusual when she, her husband, and the priest prayed together at intermission time?

"I felt something pass through me. Moreover, that night I slept like a baby, the first time in two weeks that I had been able to sleep at all."

Was the once-evident then-vanished lump a miraculous cure or a missed diagnosis? A true healing through faith-filled prayer or a purely natural phenomenon? A divine intervention or a human accident?

* * *

I could not begin to count the number of times that people have come to me as a priest and sought my prayers to relieve some burden they carried or solve a problem they faced. Up until a few years ago, my response would have been to show a compassionate concern, promise my prayers, walk away, rather vaguely commend the situation to God and normally, except in particularly tragic or crucial circumstances, fail to remember the persons explicitly in prayer at all.

Reading a number of books on healing, observing contemporary developments, and reflecting on the Scriptures changed that pattern. Today, like the priest in the story at the beginning of this chapter, I would seek to manifest real compassion and agree to pray; but I would also invite the petitioner (or petitioners) here and now, on the spot, to join me in a brief spontaneous and vocal prayer for the intention mentioned. While doing so, we might join hands or I might lay my hands upon the petitioner.

Such common ordinary prayer for healing invariably touches the heart and sometimes even the body of those who request this help.

The biblical texts which altered my pastoral approach have always been there, of course; but for reasons we will see in the next chapter, many of us either ignored them or failed to see their application in our day. Nevertheless, the foundation from Scripture for such practical prayer is clear, logical, and persuasive.

We observed in the last chapter the great compassion of Jesus for those suffering in any way and how that inner pity for them led Christ to heal. "Jesus continued his tour of all the towns and villages. He taught in their synagogues, he proclaimed the good news of God's reign, and he cured every sickness and disease" (Matthew 9:35).

However, despite his divine power, Jesus was only one person, and the presence of so many in need of physical, spiritual, and emotional help caused him frustration and again stirred his compassion. "At the sight of the crowds, his heart was moved with pity. They were lying prostrate from exhaustion, like sheep without a shepherd" (Matthew 9:36).

To solve that problem by extending his healing power, Jesus summoned "twelve disciples and gave them authority to expel unclean spirits and to cure sickness and disease of every kind. . . . Jesus sent these men on mission as the Twelve, after giving them the following instructions. . . . 'As you go, make this announcement: "The reign of God is at hand." Cure the sick, raise the dead, heal the leprous, expel demons' " (Matthew 10:1-8).

Armed with that authority, power, and mission, the Twelve Apostles set forth and widened the Lord's work. "They went off, preaching the need of repentance. They expelled many demons, anointed the sick with oil, and worked many cures" (Mark 6:12-13). Later, "the apostles returned to Jesus and reported to him all that they had done and what they had taught" (Mark 6:30).

But the Twelve were limited as well and had other

tasks to perform besides caring for the sick. Consequently, Jesus took another step and created additional ministers for the hurting. "After this, the Lord appointed a further seventy-two and sent them in pairs before him to every town and place he intended to visit" (Luke 10:1).

These seventy-two disciples recall the seventy (or seventy-two) elders of the Hebrew Scriptures which God appointed to assist the overburdened Moses as he guided the Israelites through the desert to the Promised Land (Numbers 11:11-25).[1]

The seventy-two disciples, like the Twelve, were given a charge and power to carry out their task. "Into whatever city you go, after they welcome you, eat what they set before you, and cure the sick there. Say to them, 'The reign of God is at hand' " (Luke 10:8-9).

Christ thus expanded his healing ministry. However, we see a final step in this regard and one that affects all of us in the so-called longer ending of Mark's Gospel. The risen Lord there speaks to the Eleven (Judas had died and not yet been replaced) and sends them forth, adding this promise: "Signs like these will accompany those who have professed their faith: they will use my name to expel demons, they will speak entirely new languages, they will be able to handle serpents, they will be able to drink deadly poison without harm, and the sick upon whom they lay their hands will recover" (Mark 16:17-18).

This remarkable power to lay hands upon the sick who will then recover is not restricted to the Apostles or the seventy-two disciples. It is not limited to priests or consecrated religious. It is not reserved to unique healers but has been promised to all who profess their faith in Christ. It is in fact for all of us who walk in Jesus' footsteps, who believe in him, who call ourselves Christians, who use the word Catholic for our religious identity.

That simple biblical progression — Jesus to the

Apostles to the seventy-two to us — made great sense to me and slowly shifted my pastoral approach.

How do we go about this personal prayer for healing others' pains and problems?

Those with experience suggest a very uncomplicated way: Merely speak to God as you would to a friend about another friend. Do it alone or with others, quietly or aloud, with or without words, in your own terms or using phrases someone else has provided. Where feasible, don't hesitate to touch or lay hands upon the one for whom you are praying.

One couple from Texas began this type of informal family prayer a dozen years ago. They assembled their children in the living room after dinner, switched off the television, removed the phone from its hook, turned down the lights, asked each one to reflect prayerfully on the blessings or failures of the day, and then invited anyone who wished to share. The youngest, a three-year-old, was the first to respond.

The mother and father also began to trace a cross of blessing on the forehead of each child before bed or upon leaving the house. The custom caught hold. At this writing, their college-age children, home on holidays and before examination, seek that blessed sign prior to departure.

Father Francis MacNutt, an authority on the subject, has written a helpful little paperback called *The Prayer That Heals: Praying for Healing in the Family*; the book provides, among its other suggestions, these practical tips:

So, if you have never prayed with someone and put your hand upon [the individual] while you prayed, I encourage you to try it. If your child is sick, laying your hand upon the child is such a natural thing to do anyway. It should be just as natural to pray for a husband, wife or friend — once you get over that initial shyness. Holding a person's hand or putting your arm around a shoulder is such a natural gesture. If the person is sick and it can be done decently, put your hand near the affected area while you are praying.

If you do start praying with people, you should soon see enough healings take place through your touch to encourage you and strengthen your faith even more.

For instance, you may pray with a person who has a tumor and, as you put your hand upon that tumor, you may gradually see it disappear. At first, you won't be sure: Is it just your imagination? But then, as you pray, you find, to your amazement, that it really is shrinking. Usually, it just takes one or two experiences like that to convince you that God still wants ordinary people like you — simple believers — to lay hands upon the sick who will then recover.

There is one beautiful discovery about healing touch that I would especially like to share, and that is how wonderful it is for a husband (or friends) to pray for a pregnant wife and her unborn baby. Sometimes the baby gives its first kick as the mother is prayed for — life responding to life. Of course, if the mother is alone she can put her hand upon her stomach and pray for the child. A friend, Dr. Conrad Baars, says that a mother can actually play with her unborn child by placing her hand, first on one side for a while, then on the other. The baby will turn in the womb, gradually shifting around until its back is toward the mother's loving hand. Parents who have prayed for their children before birth report that these children seem to be happier, cry less and have better dispositions than their children born in previous years without such prayer.[2]

I can identify with those words, remembering well how my mother held my forehead during moments of nausea in the bathroom and having often watched a parent kiss the hurting spot of an ailing child.

47

But as Father MacNutt mentions, there can be an initial shyness, some immediate reluctance, or even a hesitant faith in the power of ordinary people's prayer to heal.

Jesuit Father Dennis Linn had that hesitancy when he conducted a thirty-day retreat for Carol, whose deafness made it necessary for her to lip-read. He resisted the inclination to step forward and pray for her physical healing. Father Linn describes below a lesson he learned the hard way through Carol:

For 30 days we met for one hour each day. During this time I felt that, if I were to pray with her about her deafness, her hearing could be restored. But what if I prayed with Carol and her hearing wasn't restored? Her faith might be weakened, making it difficult during the retreat for Carol to trust God, let alone to trust her retreat director.

Day after day, as I directed Carol, I entertained many thoughts of praying with her for a restoration of her hearing. At times I would consider how miracles happened only in the early Church, when atheists needed the witness value of miracles. As those thoughts drifted by, I would thank God that our generation was beyond needing miracles of physical healing. I rationalized about how fortunate Carol and I were because her deafness could call both of us to greater faith.

Yet, on other days, I could convince myself that maybe God would heal small things like my upset stomach, but probably nothing as big as deafness. I remembered a few times when I did pray about "big" things such as cancer and not much change had taken place. In one instance, the person was inconsiderate enough to die on me — and I wasn't prepared to experience another "failure."

Because I feared failing and had lost confidence in Jesus working through my prayers, I started thinking of ways in which Carol might be healed. I could concede that Jesus might heal Carol's condition only if she went to a special place such as Lourdes or Fatima, or only if she had someone special like Kathryn Kuhlman pray with her. My 12 years of intellectual seminary training came in handy as I imagined ways that Jesus might heal Carol, ways which would not involve me.

For 30 days I struggled, trying to involve myself in facing Carol's deafness with her. In the end, my fears won out. I failed to discuss her condition, avoided praying with her about it, and she left the retreat as physically deaf as she came in.

Even though I had given up, Carol had not. A year later I received a letter from her telling me: "I can hear dripping water, people behind me, birds, wind. . . . It is all like music." She had asked some friends to pray over her and her hearing was totally restored! Jesus ignored all my tip-toeing around; he healed Carol without demanding that she find Kathryn Kuhlman or journey to Lourdes. Carol's physicians confirmed that her hearing was normal, despite the fact that she still has the same physical damage (genetic neural defect with auditory nerve damage). Four years have passed and Carol continues to hear normally — even while carrying on phone conversations with her chicken-hearted retreat director.[3]

Father Linn, something of a skeptic about healing before his experience with Carol, is no longer one. He and his brother have given themselves, with permission of their Jesuit superiors, full time to this ministry. However, there still exist many today — as there were yesterday — who have difficulties with or raise objections about healing in our modern world.

5

Present and Past Obstacles

Aaron Kushner was a bright and happy child who at the age of two could identify different kinds of dinosaurs and explain with patience to inquiring adults that dinosaurs were extinct.

However, his father (a Jewish rabbi) and his mother had been concerned about the tiny tot's health from earliest days, particularly when he stopped gaining weight at eight months and when he began losing hair after one year.

Distinguished doctors examined the boy and put a complicated scientific name to his condition; they assured the anxious parents that Aaron would grow to be very short but otherwise quite normal.

Around the time of his third birthday, the family moved to a Boston suburb where Rabbi Kushner assumed responsibility for a local congregation. There the parents learned of a pediatrician researching problems connected with the growth of children and asked for his analysis of Aaron's situation.

Several months later, the specialist informed them that their child had progeria, or "rapid aging." The doctor more specifically predicted "that Aaron would never grow much beyond three feet in height, would have no hair on his head or body, would look like a little old man while he was still a child, and would die in his early teens."

Aaron in fact died two days after his fourteenth birthday, leaving behind sorrowful, angry parents with many unanswered questions about a good God who could afflict such pain upon people or fail to cure such a cruel disease.[1]

* * *

To ponder the possibility of divine intervention dissolving the lump on Jane's breast or to wonder about the failure of God to heal Aaron Kushner's rare disease raises two fundamental questions: (1) Can and does God enter our lives in these modern times and work miracles by curing illnesses? (2) If God can and does bring about true healings, why are some people, like Jane, so blessed and others, like Aaron, not?

We will deal with the first question below and the second issue in a subsequent chapter.

Morton Kelsey, former rector of an Episcopalian church in California and currently a professor at the University of Notre Dame, nationwide author and lecturer on healing, writes and speaks on the subject, not merely from scholarly research but also from personal experience. He comments in his introduction to *Healing and Christianity*: "I am certainly not a paragon of physical health, nor am I unusually gifted as a healer. But I have experienced the effects of healing in my own life, ministered by another, and I have also seen the quickening power of new health come to some of those to whom I have ministered. I have seen the things of which I write."[2]

Kelsey maintains that most modern Christian religious bodies not only reject official involvement with a ministry which heals the sick but are openly hostile to the idea that healing might or ought to take place within the Church.[3] While he may have more recently altered his position, first published in 1973, many people still harbor that hostility, and the reasons noted in his book for such rejection of contemporary healing supply us with a framework for our discussion.[4]

• *Modern medicine can do it all.* The rapid, radical, and wonderful development of medicine in this century has been a mixed blessing. We see enormous progress in eliminating or alleviating human suffering; but we also can recognize a false emphasis upon and near-deification of medical science.

In earlier times, when medicine concentrated almost totally upon physical or material organs and processes in its efforts, there was obviously no room for a spiritual dimension to the healing process. Clergy came to support people or prepare them for death, not to make any significant contribution to the patient's recovery.

During the past three or four decades, medicine has come to understand more clearly the impact of mind and emotions upon our physical well-being. But this relationship is so complex and requires such expert knowledge that many in the medical profession often dismiss the possibility of nonmedical help for healing. Thus, they would attribute little healing value to the prayer of believing Christians.

Over the last dozen years, I have detected a softening of this approach. More and more medical professionals recognize the value of prayer in the healing process. Nevertheless, the attitude that modern medicine has all the answers and that healing is exclusively a medical matter obviously militates against prayer for healing.

• *God sends sufferings to bring about our repentance and purify our faith.* Kelsey cites well-used (at least until recently) official prayer books for the Church of England and Episcopal Church in America which reflect that approach and speak about illness or suffering as "God's visitation," "fatherly correction," and "a chastisement of the Lord." This visitation, correction, or chastisement according to those texts has been sent by God to strengthen our faith, make our repentance for sin more serious, and test our patience.

In a word, that attitude judges God to be responsible for sickness. It makes disease, illness, or misfortune into something good since through them we either are led to turn from our evil ways or grow more patient under adversity as Job and Jesus did.

Our prayer, then, according to this concept, should ask not for healing but for wisdom to understand and courage to bear this trial.

We continue to hear that view often expressed even today by sick persons or by those who care about the ill individuals. Why did God send this misfortune? How could God do that to me? What sin did I commit to warrant such punishment?

During Aaron Kushner's illness and premature death, his parents often reflected on those questions. To quote the words of Aaron's father, Rabbi Harold Kushner: "Like most people, my wife and I had grown up with an image of God as an all-wise, all-powerful parent figure who would treat us as our earthly parents did, or even better. If we were obedient and deserving, He would reward us. If we got out of line, He would discipline us, reluctantly but firmly. He would protect us from being hurt or from hurting ourselves, and would see to it that we got what we deserved in life."[5]

But their ponderings left them unsatisfied with this attitude about a good God sending misery into the world and prompted the rabbi eventually to write a best-selling book on the topic. *When Bad Things Happen to Good People* was written "for all those people who wanted to go on believing but whose anger at God made it hard for them to hold on to their faith and be confronted by religion" and "for all those people whose love for God and devotion to Him led them to blame themselves for their suffering and persuade themselves that they deserved it."[6]

One of the very positive contributions of Rabbi Kushner's book is the clear and forceful manner with which it shows how often we falsely blame God for tragedies or sickness that we humans in one way or another inflict upon ourselves. That is a partial and major answer to the question of how a good God supposedly sends bad things to good people.

Even though many good things often do happen as a result of an illness or suffering — sinners may change their ways; unbelievers may open themselves to faith; healthy relatives, friends, or health-care personnel may grow in charity as they tend to an ailing person's needs — it would be erroneous to say God wants, desires, or sends such misfortunes.

As we noted earlier, Jesus, God's Son, had a real hostility toward sickness and the forces behind it. He sought to eliminate suffering, not encourage or promote it. Christ prayed that the cup of affliction be taken away, although when that did not occur, he courageously and patiently endured it. The Master served and continues to serve as a model for us in this regard.

• *Healing miracles happened only in the early days of Christianity to establish the Church and promote preaching of the Gospel.* Both Martin Luther and John Calvin held that view, which is technically termed "dispensationalism."

Luther wrote: "Now that the apostles have preached the Word and have given their writings, and nothing more than what they have written remains to be revealed, no new and special revelation or miracle is necessary."[7]

Calvin taught: "The gift of healing disappeared with the other miraculous powers which our Lord was pleased to give for a time, that it might render the new preaching of the gospel forever wonderful."[8]

Closer to our day, theologian Karl Barth holds a similar but more refined and less definitive opinion.

However, two contemporary Catholic observers of or participants in the present healing revival going on within the charismatic renewal think differently. They see a real connection between dispensationalism and modern times and discussed that link in a recent Catholic newspaper article.

Jesuit Father Paul Quay of Chicago's Loyola University and Father Francis Martin of the Mother of God Community in Washington, D.C., drew parallels between miracles helping the early Church preach to a pagan audience and today's healings in a godless civilization.

Such healings, according to Quay, serve a specific purpose. "Whenever the Church will go out to pagans," he told the *Register*, "then you get signs and wonders. That's true even today." The reason for the resurfacing of healing by prayer is, according to this view, a commentary on modern times. "When have you found a civilization as pagan as ours?" Quay asked. "Every other civilization has had something bigger than the individual."

"A lot of healing takes place in preaching the Gospel. It's a dimension of preaching the Gospel and it gives the Good News credibility," said Father Martin. Martin said that in 1978, when he spent several months preaching in India, people he prayed over were relieved of physical problems ranging from a severed nerve to ordinary asthma. He said that these healings were an "audio-visual aid" to give people graphic evidence of God's love.

"Much of what you see today," Martin continued, "is apostolic healing, even though it's to Christians, for we've become de-Christianized. What we're dealing with in the Church are baptized non-believers. They don't know the Lord, and their lives aren't different from those of pagans."

Quay of Loyola also thinks that witnessing healing can have enormous value for Christians who are just beginning to believe or are immature in their faith or psychologically damaged. "If the Lord fills them with affirmation of how much He loves them," Quay said, "gradually they will uncoil and walk on their own and then there will be no more healings."[9]

• *God did not, does not, and cannot break into or interrupt the world of nature around us.* This represents probably the most serious contemporary obstacle or objection to the power of prayer to bring about healing.

Well-known, respected, and followed theologians or philosophers have maintained this view or an opinion very similar to it. Kelsey cites as proponents names like Kierkegaard, Sartre, Bonhoeffer, Tillich, Bultmann, England's Bishop Robinson and America's Bishop Pike, Hamilton, Altizer, and Van Buren.

According to Kelsey, these people propose a Christian existentialism and/or "God is dead" approach to our world. He summarizes some of their views in this way: "Any idea of supernatural nonphysical reality existing apart from personal psychic material is discarded. The value of history is questioned, and a scientific understanding of the world as a closed system of reality is accepted as axiomatic. The course of nature cannot be broken into or interrupted by any powers beyond 'existence': instead meaning comes to men as they authentically live in this immediate, conscious situation. They then discover the ground of their being."[10]

Thus, God in that philosophy cannot break or interrupt the course of nature. Nor has God done so in the past. Biblical stories of miracles or healings are "myths" which must be reevaluated if we are to understand properly Jesus and the early Christians.

Kelsey describes this further development, most famously espoused by Rudolf Bultmann, with these words:

This theology is quite satisfied that there is no basis for Christian healing in the known world. It would be a typical example of intervention into the natural order by supernatural powers, a break-through that changes the foregone conclusion. Bultmann, who is the clearest and most consistent representative of this school, views the Gospel account of healing as "mythology." These events, he holds, did not take place in actual fact, but were created by the faith of the early Christian community. Even the resurrection experience was a result of that faith rather than a fact in the strictest sense.

In order for modern man to accept the Christian message, the kerygma, Bultmann finds it necessary to demythologize the early Christian documents. Only then can we appreciate Jesus Christ and experience the power of the early Christian community.

From this point of view all angels and demons, all extrasensory knowledge, the experiences of prophecy and tongues, the value of dreams and visions, as well as every account of healing the demon-possessed and the physically ill, must simply be rejected. They did not happen as such. Obviously, since they did not happen then, there is no reason to believe that they happen now. If one believes that they do, or that they should, it is because he is still under the domination of a "mythological" point of view which is untenable in the modern world. Christian healing, therefore, has no place in today's Christianity, which is dealing with men where they are. It need not be considered, and any modern accounts of it are probably distortions of fact.[11]

Most people do not like to be called outdated, old school, or out of touch with the modern world and modern thought. Consequently, the arguments of Bultmann and his later supporters have had great practical impact upon current attitudes about healing. One does not easily oppose such a popular trend or powerful thinker. As a result, those who believe in or have received healing may feel reluctant to speak their views or share their experiences. Moreover, testimonies about cures make adherents of the "demythologize theology" thrust uncomfortable, to say the least.

In trying to reconcile the pain and tragedy of Aaron's life and death with his own belief in a good, loving God, Rabbi Kushner seems to have adopted this view that God did not, does not, and cannot break into or interrupt the course of nature.

He writes: "I believe in God. But I do not believe the same things about Him that I did years ago when I was growing up or when I was a theological student. I recognize His limitations. He is limited in what He can do by laws of nature and by the evolution of human nature and human moral freedom. I no longer hold God responsible for illnesses, accidents, and natural disasters, because I realize that I gain little and I lose so much when I blame God for those things. I can worship a God who hates suffering but cannot eliminate it, more easily than I can worship a God who chooses to make children suffer and die, for whatever exalted reason.

"God does not cause our misfortunes. Some are caused by bad luck, some are caused by bad people, and some are simply an inevitable consequence of our being human and being mortal, living in a world of inflexible natural laws."[12]

Rabbi Kushner adds, "Fate, not God, sends us the problem."[13] Presumably, then, fate, not God, also sends the solution. Since God has nothing to do with or can do nothing about the entrance of sufferings in our lives, he therefore — to carry out the logic of Kushner's views —

has nothing to do with the removal of sufferings or can do nothing about them.

A Catholic moral theology professor maintains an almost identical view when she asserts, "There is no causal link between God and the premoral evils which cause humankind so much suffering." Furthermore, blessings which believers attribute to God belong to the category of "random good fortune rather than a genre of minor miracles."[14]

God is somehow — as I interpret Rabbi Kushner and the theology instructor — present in our world and lives but does not alter the course of nature for better or for worse on our behalf.

These obstacles to healings in the Church are real and held by many — particularly, in our day, the last objection. But all of them must cope with a major difficulty. They face a Catholic Church tradition which from the very beginning believed, and continues to believe to this day, in God's intervention with humankind — which holds that prayer somehow, even though mysteriously, can bring about spiritual and physical healing, and which has and does provide rich and beautiful liturgical rituals for healing of the sick, the dying, and those in any way hurting.

6

A Long and Continuous Tradition

"Once, when Peter and John were going up to the temple for prayer at the three o'clock hour, a man crippled from birth was being carried in. They would bring him every day and put him at the temple gate called 'the Beautiful' to beg from the people as they entered. When he saw Peter and John on their way in, he begged them for an alms. Peter fixed his gaze on the man; so did John. 'Look at us!' Peter said. The cripple gave them his whole attention, hoping to get something. Then Peter said: 'I have neither silver nor gold, but what I have I give you! In the name of Jesus Christ the Nazorean, walk!' Then Peter took him by the right hand and pulled him up. Immediately the beggar's feet and ankles became strong; he jumped up, stood for a moment, then began to walk around. He went into the temple with them — walking, jumping about, and praising God. When the people saw him moving and giving praise to God, they recognized him as that beggar who used to sit at the Beautiful Gate of the temple. They were struck with astonishment — utterly stupefied at what had happened to him" (Acts 3:1-10).

"At Lystra there was a man who was lame from birth; he used to sit crippled, never having walked in his life. On one occasion he was listening to Paul preaching, and Paul looked directly at him and saw that he had the faith to be saved. He called out to him in a loud voice, 'Stand up! On your feet!' The man jumped up and began to walk around" (Acts 14:8-10).

* * *

We saw in Chapter 4 how the Twelve Apostles — charged by Jesus with the mission and given the authority to cure the sick, raise the dead, heal the leprous, and expel demons — went off and did just that, sometimes if not always anointing the ill with oil (see Matthew 10:1-8; Mark 6:7-13).

The two stories at the beginning of this chapter, taken from the Acts of the Apostles, describe how those twin pillars of the early Church, Peter and Paul, continued the carrying out of that mercy mission to hurting people during the first decades of Christianity. While neither incident mentions the laying on of hands or the anointing with oil, we can presume from different episodes recorded in Scripture and transmitted by tradition that they and other leaders made these elements a standard feature of their healing ministry.

It would have been a surprise if they did not, particularly in the case of the anointing with oil, since during those days this was a common procedure.

At the time of Jesus and even before that, people used oil (especially olive oil) for many purposes — some merely practical and others quite religious. Among its many uses, oil was employed for cooking and eating, for the lighting of lamps, for a cleansing substance in bathing similar to soap today, for cosmetics and healing medicines, for protection against the dry climate, for a symbol of joy, for a sign of respect, and for preparation of the dead.

Jewish tradition, perhaps absorbing a custom from the surrounding Egyptian and Canaanite cultures, also developed the practice of anointing persons and objects with oil, thereby setting them aside for religious or sacred use. Thus, to illustrate, the Hebrew Scriptures tell us priests, prophets, and kings were anointed and by that action consecrated to God's service.[1]

This Jewish tradition of oil anointing consequently crept into the practices of primitive Christianity as we see recorded in the excerpt from Mark's Gospel cited in Chapter 4. When Pope Paul VI, some nineteen hundred years later, introduced the *Rite of Anointing and Pastoral Care of the Sick* (a ritual revised according to the directives of the Second Vatican Council), the Holy Father referred to that text from Mark. Repeating the Catholic Church's teaching that anointing of the sick is one of the New Testament's seven sacraments, the Holy Father said that it was instituted by Christ our Lord and "intimated in Mark."

The incident recorded in Mark 6:7-13 suggests, insinuates, or intimates this sacrament which, according to Paul VI, was subsequently "recommended" and "made known" to believers through James, one of the Apostles and often called brother of the Lord.[2]

That excerpt from the Epistle of James is the classic biblical passage employed to establish and explain the sacrament of anointing of the sick and is also used frequently within celebrations of the rite itself: "If anyone among you is suffering hardship, he must pray. If a person is in good spirits, he should sing a hymn of praise. Is there anyone sick among you? He should ask for the presbyters of the Church. They in turn are to pray over him, anointing him with oil in the Name [of the Lord]. This prayer uttered in faith will reclaim the one who is ill, and the Lord will restore him to health. If he has committed any sins, forgiveness will be his. Hence, declare your sins to one another, and pray for one another, that you may find healing" (James 5:13-16).

By carefully studying the words of that paragraph in

their original language and cultural setting, we can arrive at these conclusions about how the early Church ministered this sacrament to the sick:

• The sick person was probably ill enough to be confined to bed but not necessarily in a grave condition or near death.

• The illness very likely was a bodily infirmity. However, since the Jewish mind in those days didn't distinguish body and spirit or separate sin from sickness, James was speaking about a completely sick person — body and spirit — whose restoration would also be complete, total, whole, and entire.

• Those to be called were apparently neither bishops, priests, or deacons as we know them today nor the charismatic healers mentioned in St. Paul's Letter to the Corinthians ("Through the Spirit one receives faith; by the same Spirit another is given the gift of healing, and still another miraculous powers" — 1 Corinthians 12:9-10). Instead they were seemingly people with an official position of authority in the local church, officeholders, or officially recognized ministers.

• The visitors prayed not for but over the sick person, gathering around and perhaps even laying hands upon the ill individual.

• The presbyters anointed the infirm person with oil, although more importance appeared to be given to the prayer of faith than to this action of anointing.

• The healing presence and power of Jesus was called upon, indicating the restoration expected was not merely a physical or medical cure but a spiritual one as well.

• As a result of this visitation or intervention, the sick person could expect both a bodily or medical healing as well as a spiritual restoration. The ritual would touch the entire religious situation of the ill individual. That included salvation from sin, eventual resurrection from the dead, as well as recovery of health. The positive effects of the prayer and anointing would be limited neither to spiritual or physical healing but would extend to both.

- If a person had serious sins, the sins would be forgiven. This was a conditional effect, because the infirm one did not need to be in a state of serious sinfulness.[3]

The action described or recommended by James clearly foreshadowed what was to become the practice of the Church over ensuing centuries and is our own today. As might be expected, however, the history of anointing in the Church, while continuous, nevertheless remains vague, particularly during early years, and has experienced several shifts in emphasis over the centuries.

In general, we see at the beginning a concentration upon the sacrament as one intended primarily for healing the sick; then the main thrust came to consider this as a rite or sacrament for the dying; finally, in recent centuries and our own day, there has been a gradual return to considering the sacrament of anointing with oil as primarily concerned about healing the hurting. The preparation-for-dying aspect has been taken up by viaticum, or communion for the sick, under a special formula.

- For the first eight hundred years, there is every indication from the writings of Church Fathers, liturgical documents, and lives of the saints that the Church anointed those who were sick. However, we are not absolutely clear about the way this was done, other than to note these salient elements: (1) The oil, presented by the faithful, was blessed by the bishop. That blessing, viewed as the most important part of the rite, gave the oil a divine power and placed it in the category of a sacrament. (2) The application of the oil was entrusted not only to the presbyters but likewise to lay persons who would anoint themselves, sick relatives, and ill friends. (3) A prayer of some sort normally accompanied the anointing as did usually the laying on of hands. (4) People applied the oil externally but also might at times take it internally by consuming it. (5) The anointing was not seen as a preparation for death but as a ritual to restore bodily and spiritual health.[4]

• From the ninth century until the Council of Trent in the sixteenth, a radical shift occurred in the use of this anointing rite. It became a sacrament for the dying instead of a ritual to restore health. More specifically: (1) The anointing itself was restricted to presbyters or priests. (2) A more formal ritual evolved with precise prayers to be recited. (3) Priests began to anoint the five senses — eyes, ears, nose, mouth, hands — and to join each anointing with a prayer which linked it with the forgiveness of sins; for example, "May the Lord forgive you by this holy anointing and this most loving mercy, whatever sins you have committed by the use of your sight, etc. Amen." (4) The anointing was connected with deathbed conversions and began to be viewed as a sacrament for the dying. (5) The sacrament came to be called "Extreme Unction," or the last anointing, since it was the final anointing to be received in this life and before death. (6) The order for the sick shifted from penance, anointing, and viaticum to penance, viaticum, and anointing. (7) The principal effect sought was no longer the restoration of health but a preparation for the glory of heaven after death. (8) Extreme Unction, also unhappily becoming known as "the last rites," was seen to remove our sins and the remnants of our sins, strengthen us in the final battle, and speed our passage to God after death.[5]

• The period from the Council of Trent until the Second Vatican Council saw a gradual but not complete return to the practice of James and the early Church: (1) The Council of Trent providentially did not continue the restrictions of the earlier period. On the contrary, it said that the sacrament was to be given "especially" — instead of "only" — to those who are so dangerously ill that they seem close to death. (2) It confirmed that priests were the proper ministers of the sacrament. (3) It upheld the teaching that this was a true sacrament, one of the seven, and traced its origin to Christ through Mark and James. (4) It listed, without priority, the triple effects of this sacrament: to take away sin and its remains; to strengthen the sick person inwardly or spiritually during the struggle of sickness and dying; to restore bodily health when that will prove beneficial for the welfare of the entire person. This particular teaching most significantly opened up the possibility of returning to the original practice within the Church. (5) During the centuries following Trent, Church practice became more and more lenient in its interpretation of what "danger of death" meant and also stressed the health-restoring power of the sacrament. (6) Popes during the twentieth century frequently urged those who care for the seriously sick and dying to summon the priest early for this sacrament so that its beneficial effects might be received by the ill individual. (7) Nevertheless, the concept of "last rites" perdured and Catholics in general continued to fear the sacrament. Family, friends, or medical personnel would only with reluctance summon the clergy. Such a call seemed to indicate that all hope had gone and certain death lay ahead.[6]

• That slow reversal, however, set the stage for the treatment of this sacrament by the bishops gathered at Rome during the 1960s for the Second Vatican Council. In the "Constitution on the Sacred Liturgy" (paragraphs 72-75), they decreed the following: (1) "Extreme Unction" more fittingly should be called "Anointing of the Sick." (2) It is not a sacrament only for those at the point of death. (3) As soon as anyone begins to be in danger of death from sickness or old age, it is fitting to anoint the person. (4) The continuous order for the seriously ill is restored to penance, anointing, and viaticum. (5) The number of anointings and the prayers were to be revised to correspond better to today's varying needs.[7]

The fruit of those brief paragraphs (72-75) in the "Constitution on the Sacred Liturgy" was the restored *Rite of Anointing and Pastoral Care of the Sick*, issued by Pope Paul VI in 1972. We will examine this rich ritual in the next chapter.

7

Mending Wounded Hearts and Bodies

When Bishop Odore Gendron brought together all the priests of his Manchester, New Hampshire, diocese for a four-day convocation, he wished to promote through this gathering a closer bond among the clergy. During that time some two hundred fifty men listened to lectures, prayed together, spent the afternoons in relaxation, and visited over meals, at social hours, during walks, or in small informal talk sessions.

The bishop hoped that as a result of this unique undertaking these priests would come to know one another better, be closer to one another, and share more easily their common burdens, successful pastoral practices, and spiritual victories.

His dream came true, but one of the most powerful events which helped realize that goal developed quite unexpectedly.

Three seriously ill priests arrived at the conference not out of any obligation but simply through a desire to join their brothers. One of them stood out because of his cane, emaciated body, jaundiced skin, and lost hair — visible effects of a rampant cancer and the radical therapy designed to cure it.

With such critically sick men present, the convocation leaders decided after some discussion to modify the schedule and celebrate an evening healing service combining the sacrament for the anointing of the sick with the sacrament of penance.

The three men agreed to be anointed, and five others then came forward asking to receive this sacrament as well.

After an opening hymn and prayer plus appropriate scriptural readings with a brief homily, Bishop Gendron led the assembly in a litany which contained the petition: "Give life and health to our brothers on whom we lay our hands in your name. . . ."

Following that invocation, the eight ill men moved to a slightly elevated platform and sat down facing the community. For the next half hour, their two hundred fifty brother-priests, including the bishop, silently and slowly filed by these men, and with great care and deep emotion, gently laid hands upon each one.

There were noticeable tears among many, and not so visible but equally profound inner stirrings among all — for these sick men had baptized a few of the priests, were classmates of some, had worked with, helped, and hurt still others.

When the last priest had passed by, the eight men stood up and in turn laid hands upon one another, often with embraces which touched the onlookers.

Bishop Gendron proceeded to anoint each man with the sacramental oil and, in conclusion, read this prayer: "Father in heaven, through this holy anointing grant these men, our brothers, comfort in their suffering. When they are afraid, give them courage; when afflicted, give them patience; when dejected, afford them hope; and when alone, assure them of the support of your holy people."

The priest with the cane stood up following that prayer and said:

"I want to thank you men, not so much for the laying

on of your hands or for this anointing sacrament, but for something else. You know from your own priestly ministry how — when people are dying — their relatives and friends often treat them as if they have the plague or an infectious disease and stay away. You have not treated us that way, and did not tonight. On behalf of the eight of us, I thank you for that."

These words brought the entire community to its feet, and the sustained applause which ensued expressed sentiments of the heart too complex, diversified, and intimate to describe.

Afterward, about twenty priests were available for the sacrament of penance, and for over two hours several heard confessions of the clergy present.

One of the participants, moved by the healing ceremony, went to the room of the priest with the cane and spoke with him for half an hour, begging his forgiveness for a misunderstanding of the past.

These men indeed shared one another's burdens that night.

* * *

Soon after Pope Paul VI issued the official Latin text for the revised rite for the anointing and pastoral care of the sick in 1972, the American bishops, among others, approved a provisional English translation of the document and published a new ritual for use by priests of the United States in serving those who are ill.

After a decade of experience with that book, the conference of bishops in this country produced a finalized version containing considerable adaptations suggested by those who had employed the initial volume. The 1982 publication *Pastoral Care of the Sick: Rites of Anointing and Viaticum* reflects the Church's current approach to this matter not only by its actual content but also through its title and format.[1]

Pastoral Care of the Sick thus contains two distinct

70

liturgical elements: a rite of anointing and a rite for viaticum. Part I ("Pastoral Care of the Sick") includes visitation, communion, and anointing of the sick. Part II ("Pastoral Care of the Dying") contains the ritual for viaticum, commendation of the dying, and prayers for the dead.

By that division, the Church clearly teaches that anointing today is more a sacrament of healing and support for the sick rather than a ritual for the dying. Moreover, it indicates that viaticum — communion with a special format and formula — is the Church's official rite for those in danger of or near death.

In this chapter, various aspects of the rite for the anointing of the sick will be explained. In subsequent sections, we will examine the Church's rituals for visiting the sick and providing them with communion as well as the Church's liturgical support for the dying.

The Church's Approach to Sickness

In its general introduction to the rites for Part I ("Pastoral Care of the Sick"), the Church urges a double thrust with regard to illness: Do all we can to overcome sickness but be patient throughout unavoidable sufferings. Thus, "Part of the plan laid out by God's providence is that we should fight strenuously against all sickness and carefully seek the blessings of good health so that we may fulfill our role in human society and in the Church. Yet we should always be prepared to fill up what is lacking in Christ's sufferings for the salvation of the world as we look forward to creation's being set free in the glory of the children of God (see Colossians 1:24; Romans 8:19-21)."[2]

To help achieve that goal, the ceremonies, readings, and prayers for Part I of this ritual text (including the rite of anointing) have as their purpose "to comfort the sick in time of anxiety, to encourage them to fight against illness, and perhaps restore them to health."[3]

The Effects of Anointing

The sacrament of anointing of the sick provides those who are seriously ill with possibly a restoration of health and certainly the special help of God's grace in their time of anxiety "lest they be broken in spirit, and under the pressure of temptation, perhaps weakened in their faith."[4]

In the last chapter I traced the history of anointing and the shifts in emphasis which have happened over the centuries. The list of effects below, taken from the Vatican II restored ritual, will show how the Church has returned almost precisely to the position on anointing described in James 5:14-16.

As an overall effect, the Church declares that this sacrament "gives the grace of the Holy Spirit to those who are sick."

More specifically that means: (1) "By this grace the whole person is helped and saved, sustained by trust in God, and strengthened against the temptations of the Evil One and against anxiety over death. Thus the sick person is able not only to bear suffering bravely but also to fight against it." (2) "A return to health may follow the reception of this sacrament if it will be beneficial to the sick person's salvation." (3) "If necessary, the sacrament also provides the sick person with the forgiveness of sins and the completion of Christian penance."[5]

The readings, prayers, blessings, and gestures of the ritual itself naturally reflect this teaching about the effects of the sacrament. Thus:

• *"The grace of the Holy Spirit to those who are sick"*: The formula which accompanies the actual anointing with oil reads in part, "Through this holy anointing may the Lord in his love and mercy help you with the grace of the Holy Spirit."[6]

• *"To bear suffering bravely"*: Bishop Gendron

recited over those New Hampshire priests a prayer conveying that notion and asking for God's help for the sick men so that they might indeed bear their burdens bravely. Another petition, also to be used after the anointing, contains similar thoughts: "Support him/her with your power, comfort him/her with your protection, and give him/her the strength to fight against evil. Since you have given him/her a share in your own passion, help him/her to find hope in suffering."[7]

- *"A return to health"*: The blessings at the end of the ceremony include these requests: "May God the Son heal you. . . . May God restore you to health and grant you salvation."[8]
- *"The forgiveness of sins"*: A general prayer after the anointing explicitly mentions this effect. "Heal his/her sickness and forgive his/her sins; expel all afflictions of mind and body. . . ."[9]

Who Is to Be Anointed

The priest, considered by the ritual to be the only proper minister of the anointing, should be solicitous about providing this sacrament to those who need it but must also avoid an indiscriminate anointing of those who are not suitable recipients of the sacrament.[10]

The general principle determining who may be appropriately anointed is this: "Great care should be taken to see that those of the faithful whose health is seriously impaired by sickness or old age receive this sacrament."

The phrase "seriously impaired" is the key element in this norm. The sick person need not be gravely, dangerously, or perilously ailing to be eligible for the sacrament. On the other hand, people slightly ill — for example, with a minor cold or headache — are not proper candidates for anointing. Consequently, a general invitation for all present who are in any way sick to come forward and receive this sacrament would be inconsistent with the Church's current teaching and regulations.

The ritual, nevertheless, wishes the words "seriously impaired" to be interpreted liberally and without anxiety. "A prudent and reasonably sure judgment, without scruple, is sufficient for deciding on the seriousness of an illness; if necessary a doctor may be consulted."[11]

Here are some practical applications of the general norm to common situations: (1) "The sacrament may be repeated if the sick person recovers after being anointed and then again falls ill or if during the same illness the person's condition becomes more serious." (2) "In the case of a person who is chronically ill, or elderly and in a weakened condition, the sacrament of anointing may be repeated when in the pastoral judgment of the priest the condition of the sick person warrants the repetition of the sacrament." (3) A sick person may be anointed before surgery whenever a serious illness is the reason for the surgery. (4) Elderly people may be anointed if they have become notably weakened even though no serious illness is present. (5) Sick children may be anointed if they have sufficient use of reason to be strengthened by this sacrament. (6) The sacrament of anointing may be conferred upon sick people who, although they have lost consciousness or the use of reason, would, as Christian believers, probably have asked for it were they in control of their faculties. (7) When a priest has been called to attend those who are already dead, he should not administer the sacrament of anointing. Instead, he should pray for them, asking that God forgive their sins and graciously receive them into the kingdom. But if the priest is doubtful whether the sick person is dead, he may give the sacrament conditionally. (8) Some types of mental sickness are now classified as serious. Those who are judged to have a serious mental illness and who would be strengthened by the sacrament may be anointed. The anointing may be repeated in accordance with the conditions for other kinds of serious illness.

The Church very strongly urges that relatives, friends, or health-care personnel summon the priest early on in a serious illness so that the sick individual may receive the sacrament "with full faith and devotion."[12]

The Actual Anointing

Pope Paul VI decreed that the essential sacramental rite consists of anointing the seriously ill on the forehead and hands with blessed olive oil or another blessed plant oil while saying these words:

(While anointing the forehead) "Through this holy anointing may the Lord in his love and mercy help you with the grace of the Holy Spirit."

(While anointing the hands) "May the Lord who frees you from sin save you and raise you up."

In case of necessity, however, the priest may give a single anointing on the forehead or, because of the sick person's particular condition, on another suitable part of the body (such as the general area of pain or injury).[13]

Prayer of Faith

There was a general tendency before the Second Vatican Council to give the sacrament of anointing an almost automatic and magiclike power. The family and/or health-care personnel often delayed summoning the priest until the sick person was unconscious and nearly dead. Moreover, upon the priest's arrival these people generally left the room or, if they remained, merely stood back, frozen in their fears. Meanwhile, the priest recited a few prayers quietly next to the ailing one and signed with oil all the senses of the critically ill individual. The participants possessed a certain faith, enough at least to call the priest and to believe in God's power working through these sacred words and gestures. However, the patient and those present had little opportunity to express or deepen their faith.

Jesus, as we have seen, did on occasion heal persons without faith; but usually belief was a condition for the cure or a reason behind it. Moreover, his wondrous deeds had as their ultimate goal to bring people to faith in him and his message.

The Church, with its reformed ritual, wishes to resurrect that approach and to stress the importance of faith for the effective celebration of this sacrament. Thus, "In the anointing of the sick, which includes the prayer of faith (see James 5:15), faith itself is manifested. Above all, this faith must be made actual both in the minister of the sacrament and, even more importantly, in the recipient. The sick person will be saved by personal faith and the faith of the Church, which looks back to the death and resurrection of Christ, the source of the sacrament's power (see James 5:15), and looks ahead to the future kingdom that is pledged in the sacraments."[14]

There are several pragmatic ways in which this faith dimension can be more fully developed during the anointing ritual. A typical situation in the ministry of Father Neal Quartier should illustrate this.

Father Quartier serves as Catholic chaplain at the Upstate Medical Center, a large state-operated hospital in Syracuse, which draws patients, particularly seriously ill persons, from all over central New York.

Providing there is time, the young priest would first seek to become acquainted with the patient and the family, as well as speak with others involved (including the health-care personnel).

In the course of his first and subsequent visits, Father Quartier would talk about the sacrament, its purpose, and the bond which exists among all members of the Church. He would emphasize that through our common faith and common baptism we are members of the body of Christ. Because of that link the sufferings of one are the sufferings of all. Our prayer and this sacrament, the chaplain would continue, is done in the name and power of Jesus and his entire Church. Thus their own faith, joined with the faith of the whole body of believers, is powerful indeed. Quartier's words would bring support and hope for both the ill individual and all who care for him or her.

He might then describe the various readings and prayers available as options for them in the anointing ceremony and set a specific time for all to be on hand.

During the actual celebration of the rite, they would, as a result, join in the prayers, hear God's word, perhaps hold or touch the sick one, and possibly sing appropriate songs. Their faith and the faith of the seriously ill patient would be expressed and deepened.

Father Quartier, at the start of the anointing would very likely read an instruction which includes these words from James, "the prayer of faith will save the sick persons, and the Lord will raise them up."[15]

Immediately before the laying on of hands, he would probably introduce a litany of petitions in this way, "My brothers and sisters, in our prayer of faith let us appeal to God for our brother/sister N."[16]

After spreading oil on forehead and hands, the chaplain — should the patient be of advanced years — in all probability would read a prayer which contains these phrases: "Keep him/her firm in faith and serene in hope so that he/she may give us all an example of patience, and joyfully witness to the power of your love."[17]

The faith dimension — reinforced by the kind of ministry which Father Quartier performs — is also enhanced when the parish community prays for the sick person at Sunday Mass. Moreover, communal celebrations with several to be anointed, a number of priests concelebrating, and an assembly of supporters present as at the New Hampshire convocation — all these things further strengthen the faith aspect of this ritual.

The Laying on of Hands

"Bishop, now that you are approaching retirement, would you do it all over again?"

A participant at Notre Dame's clergy-renewal institute posed that question to Bishop William McManus of the Fort Wayne-South Bend (Indiana) diocese at the conclusion of an informal evening exchange.

It made the bishop pause for a moment; but he then broke into a smile, nodded, and added affirmatively, "Oh, definitely. What a privilege and a joy it has been, despite the difficult moments."

Bishop McManus went on to describe two particularly joyous occasions for him, both involving oil and the laying on of hands.

The first, a repeated inspirational event, was his presiding at priesthood ordination ceremonies.

Laying hands upon men eager to begin their priestly ministry, spreading the oil of chrism over palms which would touch so many people in blessed ways, and seeing enacted before his eyes the perennially youthful, regenerating nature of the Church — all of this always has been a thrill for Bishop McManus.

The second, a more sober but equally moving experience, was his anointment with the sacrament for the sick by the priests of the diocese.

Symptoms of deteriorating health and a doctor's examination revealed recently that the bishop's heart had serious deficiencies, with arteries badly clogged and the prognosis not good at all. The physicians recommended open-heart surgery and a needed major bypass.

Just prior to the operation, Bishop McManus joined the priests of the diocese at the Notre Dame campus for their annual retreat. During the course of those days, he received the anointing of the sick in the presence of all the clergy. As the ceremony unfolded, each priest at the appropriate time came forward and individually laid hands upon the ailing man. He wept as they did so, and most of the clergy as well walked away with tears streaming down their cheeks.

Bishop McManus, through his hands, had communicated to many of those men their priestly life. Now, in return, they were praying that through their own hands the Lord would grant this dedicated shepherd needed courage, inner healing, and new life.

Over the years the Fort Wayne-South Bend bishop, like every shepherd, has had some disagreements and misunderstandings with his clergy. But any hostility or distant feelings which might have been present on that day simply melted away before the warm outpouring of love, concern, and unity.

We have seen how Jesus often healed people by laying his hands upon them or through a simple gesture of touching them. The Church in its revised ritual restores this gesture immediately before the prayer over the oil and the anointing itself.

The rubric, or directive, reads: "In silence, the priest lays his hands on the head of the sick person."[18]

A litany precedes that gesture and may include this phrase: "Give life and health to our brother/sister N., on whom we lay our hands in your name."[19]

The laying on of hands signifies that: (1) The Church is praying for the Holy Spirit to come upon the sick person. (2) The Church blesses the person as we pray for the power of God's healing grace to restore the sick individual to health or at least to strengthen him or her in time of illness. (3) The entire Church throughout the world is in solidarity with and praying for the sick person. (4) The Church is doing what Jesus did, touching or laying hands

79

upon the ill one. (5) The Church is bringing forgiveness and reconciliation. (6) The Church wishes to be present and close to the seriously ill person who often feels isolated, alone, and abandoned or rejected.[20]

Father Kevin Murphy, before he himself became totally bedridden, would invite all present during this part of the anointing ceremony to join with him in laying hands upon those whom they loved.

Anointing With Oil

In earlier sections we observed how both Mark and James mentioned the use of oil as a means and a sign of healing. The new ritual continues this practice of anointing the sick with oil to signify healing, strengthening, and the presence of the Spirit. It has a further connotation of soothing and comforting the sick and of restoring the tired and the weak. Since illness can physically and spiritually debilitate the sick person, this oil strengthens the person to fight off these detrimental effects in his or her struggle.[21]

When a priest blesses the oil within the rite, he recites the following prayer which summarizes the particular significance of oil and the general purpose of the sacrament:

God of all consolation,
you chose and sent your Son to heal the world.
Graciously listen to our prayer of faith:
send the power of your Holy Spirit, the Consoler,
into this precious oil, this soothing ointment,
this rich gift, this fruit of the earth.

Bless this oil ✠ and sanctify it for our use.

Make this oil a remedy for all who are anointed with it;
heal them in body, in soul, and in spirit,
and deliver them from every affliction.[22]

For the symbol of oil to be effective, it should be

spread in amounts generous enough to be seen and felt and also be left on, not wiped off after the anointing.[23]

This sacrament of anointing is to heal in "body, in soul, and in spirit" and to deliver the sick "from every affliction." The Church prays and hopes that through this ritual and our faith God will heal the ill person in every way — spiritually, emotionally, mentally, and physically. It wishes to mend our wounded hearts and bodies.

8

Comforting and Curing the Sick

Grace Casey served the sick for many years as a nurse; but trouble with her swollen legs made walking difficult, working impossible, and remaining confined at home nearly all of the time an eventual necessity.

Subsequently, each month the priest stopped at her house, offered an opportunity for the sacrament of penance, gave holy communion to Grace, talked with her briefly, and then moved on to visit other ailing or elderly parishioners.

Six years ago, Bud and Angela Maynard began calling — often with their children — upon Grace every Sunday. Their pastor at that time had asked this couple to begin a ministry of mercy to the sick, or more specifically, to bring the Eucharist each week to Mrs. Casey.

The Maynards' entire family normally would participate in the 9:45 Mass, receive at communion time a consecrated particle, drive their station wagon afterward a few blocks to Grace's home, read the Sunday scriptural passages to her, summarize or even play a tape of the homily, recite the ritual prayers, give her holy communion, visit with her, leave a copy of the parish bulletin, and return home.

Grace recently suffered a stroke which forced her to enter a nursing institution and sell her beloved home. The

Maynards, however, continue to visit Grace Casey. Moreover, in one of those curious twists of life, Colleen, the Maynards' oldest daughter, just out of high school, found a job as a nurse's aid in that health-care facility and often waits upon the woman she first met as a teenager accompanying her parents after Sunday Mass.

Communion to the Sick

This practice of lay persons bringing holy communion to those confined in hospitals, nursing institutions, or homes began probably a decade ago in western Europe. It resurrected an early Christian procedure whereby the faithful took consecrated particles home on Sunday and during the week gave communion to themselves, the sick, prisoners, and others unable to be present for the weekly Eucharist.

Nevertheless, because the action represented in the 1970s a radical departure from the then-current Catholic tradition, priests encountered some opposition. To facilitate introduction of the new approach in the face of such obstacles, one bishop provided his clergy with a letter to the sick person indicating that the development enjoyed episcopal approval.

The practice quickly leaped across the Atlantic to the United States and has spread with equal swiftness, so much so that we can anticipate its introduction in every vibrant parish of our country by the end of the 1980s.

The rapidity of that growth and the desirability of having such eucharistic ministers of mercy to the sick certainly led to the inclusion of recommendations about it within the revised ritual for the United States, *Pastoral Care of the Sick.*

First, introductory guidelines urge pastoral leaders to provide frequent, even daily, opportunities for communion for the sick or confined. "Priests with pastoral responsibilities should see to it that the sick or aged, even though not seriously ill or in danger of death, are given every opportunity to receive the eucharist frequently, even daily, especially during the Easter season."[1]

Next, these directives recognize that priests or pastoral staff people probably cannot handle this obligation alone. They move on, therefore, to support the appointment of additional extraordinary ministers of the Eucharist coupled with a suggestion about suitable attire. "To provide frequent communion for the sick, it may be necessary to ensure that the community has a sufficient number of ministers of communion. The communion minister should wear attire appropriate to this ministry."[2]

Finally, the norms encourage connecting the Sunday Eucharist with the community's concern and care for the sick: "The links between the community's eucharistic celebration, especially on the Lord's Day, and the communion of the sick are intimate and manifold. Besides remembering the sick in the general intercessions at Mass, those present should be reminded occasionally of the significance of communion in the lives of those who are ill: union with Christ in his struggle with evil, his prayer for the world, and his love for the Father, and union with the community from which they are separated.

"The obligation to visit and comfort those who cannot take part in the eucharistic assembly may be clearly demonstrated by taking communion to them from the community's eucharistic celebration. This symbol of unity between the community and its sick members has the deepest significance on the Lord's Day, the special day of the eucharistic assembly."[3]

The Oakland (California) Cathedral has not only introduced this practice on an extensive scale but also dramatizes the procedure during Sunday Mass. Perhaps seventy-five people assemble in the sanctuary after communion at the major liturgy, each with one or two con-secrated hosts. The presiding priest then gives them a charge or mission in words like these:

"You special ministers of mercy to the sick, go to our beloved parishioners confined to hospitals, other health-care institutions, or their homes. Mention how we care about them and give them this Sunday's message. [He summarizes the homily in a few sentences.] Tell them that we need their prayers and sufferings and that they have ours. Go, now, take to them our risen Lord in the Eucharist."

The servers lead the way out, then the eucharistic ministers of mercy follow, and, finally, the presiding priest.

In certain parishes of my own diocese of Syracuse the ministers of mercy plan their visitations so that they will coincide with the weekly televised "Mass for Shut-ins."

While these arrangements are more or less ongoing, one detects and should expect the gradual expansion of this practice on a more informal temporary basis — that is, spouse bringing holy communion home to one's spouse, parent to children, children to parents, or rela-tive to relative throughout a temporary or short-term ill-ness.

Whatever the arrangement, here are some practical details involved with implementing this system: (1) The consecrated particle should be carried in a pyx or small closed container. (2) When possible, there ought to be a table by the side of the ill person with a linen cloth, light-ed candles, and perhaps a vessel of holy water upon it. (3) If the sick person cannot receive under the form of bread, he or she may communicate under the form of wine alone. In such a case, the blood of Christ is carried in a vessel closed in such a way as to eliminate all danger of spilling. If some remains, the minister consumes the excess amount and properly purifies it.[4] (4) The eucharistic minister to the sick should be properly trained beforehand and should use a booklet containing the prayers, readings, blessings, and directions from the official ritual for "Communion of the Sick."

Prayers and blessings in that communion rite are designed to comfort and cure the sick person. They request healing of body and spirit, physical health and spiritual strength. For example,

"Lord Jesus, you give yourself to heal us and bring us strength. . . ."[5]

"May God the Son heal you."

"May he guide you and give you strength."[6]

"May the body and blood of Christ your Son be for your brother/sister N. a lasting remedy for body and soul.'"[7]

The sick and all who are to receive communion naturally recite the familiar adapted centurion's plea: "Lord, I am not worthy to receive you, but only say the word and I shall be healed."[8]

Visiting the Sick

Obviously not every visit to a sick person, either by official representatives of the Church or other concerned individuals, includes distribution of holy communion. Those indeed are special occasions, and the Church wishes us to use care in making them joyful and signs of support or concern by the Christian community for its members who are ill.[9] However, the Church also provides a theology or philosophy and a format as well as resource texts for those more ordinary calls upon sick people.

The *philosophy* or *theology* behind these visits contains several general principles:

• It urges all to *fight against disease and sickness of every kind.* The ritual puts that charge in these words: "The sick person is not the only one who should fight against illness. Doctors and all who are devoted in

86

any way to caring for the sick should consider it their duty to use all the means which in their judgment may help the sick, both physically and spiritually. In so doing, they are fulfilling the command of Christ to visit the sick, for Christ implied that those who visit the sick should be concerned for the whole person and offer both physical relief and spiritual comfort.

"If one member suffers in the Body of Christ, which is the Church, all the members suffer with that member (2 Corinthians 12:26). For this reason, kindness shown toward the sick and works of charity and mutual help for the relief of every kind of human want are held in special honor. Every scientific effort to prolong life and every act of care for the sick, on the part of any person, may be considered a preparation for the Gospel and a sharing in Christ's healing ministry."[10]

• It holds that *concern for the sick is the responsibility of all Christians.* "The concern that Christ showed for the bodily and spiritual welfare of those who are ill is continued by the Church in its ministry to the sick. This ministry is the common responsibility of all Christians, who should visit the sick, remember them in prayer, and celebrate the sacraments with them. The family and friends of the sick, doctors and others who care for them, and priests with pastoral responsibilities have a particular share in this ministry of comfort."[11]

This concern can be expressed, among other ways, in the public prayer of the Christian community. "Remembrance of the sick is especially appropriate at common worship on the Lord's Day, during the general intercessions at Mass and in the intercessions at Morning Prayer and Evening Prayer. Family members and those who are dedicated to the care of the sick should be remembered on these occasions as well."[12]

• It recommends that *both the sick person and those who visit or care for the sick pray often, with their prayer drawn primarily from Scripture.* That prayer will seek for the one who is ill (as well as his or her family) understanding during dark days, comfort in discouragement, recovery of health, and strength throughout the struggle.[13]

• It encourages the sick and his or her loved ones to *unite and offer the sufferings in union with Christ for the good of the Church and the world.*[14] "Through words of encouragement and faith" those who call upon the sick can help the infirm "to unite themselves with the sufferings of Christ for the good of God's people."[15] Suggesting certain particular needs of the moment — for example, world peace; people suffering in a disaster; renewal of the parish — can give this intercessory suffering added meaning.

• It recalls to the sick and all others that such *diseases, illnesses, and eventual deaths are reminders of essential, higher, and eternal realities.* Our mortal lives ultimately need transformation or salvation and make sense only in terms of being redeemed by Jesus' death and resurrection.[16]

• It suggests that *those who regain their health give thanks to God* for this grace and favor by participating in a Mass of thanksgiving or through some other suitable means.[17]

The *format* for a liturgical visit to the ill provided by the ritual *Pastoral Care of the Sick* includes a reading from Scripture, a brief period of silent reflection, a psalm response, the Lord's Prayer, a concluding petition, and a blessing with the laying on of hands by the priest.

It also contains a special format for visits to a sick child, which is similar to the one just described except for prayers tailored to the situation and the addition of a sign of the cross made on the child's forehead by the visiting official minister as well as each one present.

The formulas for these visits to children are especially powerful and appropriate.

For example, after the scriptural reading, the ritual gives a simple response to be recited first by the official minister and then by those present:

Minister: "Jesus, come to me." *All present:* "Jesus, come to me."

Minister: "Jesus, put your hand on me." *All present:* "Jesus, put your hand on me."

Minister: "Jesus, bless me." *All present:* "Jesus, bless me."[18]

A concluding prayer petitions God the Father:

God of love,
ever caring,
ever strong,
stand by us in our time of need.

Watch over your child N. who is sick,
look after him/her in every danger,
and grant him/her your healing and peace.

We ask this in the name of Jesus the Lord.[19]

For the final blessing, the official minister makes a sign of the cross on the child's forehead and recites the following or similar prayer:

N., when you were baptized,
you were marked with the cross of Jesus.
I (we) make this cross ✠ on your forehead
and ask the Lord to bless you,
and restore you to health.[20]

The *resource texts*, some of which have been cited above, are extensive and include readings, responses, and verses from sacred Scripture as well as multiple blessings and prayers.

The ordinary person who calls upon a sick individual — relative, loved one, neighbor, or colleague — normally feels some uneasiness before and during the visit, especially if the condition is serious or ominous.

Beforehand we may say to ourselves, "What will I do or say when I get inside the room?" Once actually standing or sitting next to the ill individual, we may question ourselves again, "How will I respond? Is there something I can do? Are there words I should say?"

While using the prayers and readings from the revised ritual certainly is a possibility and highly desirable, most people I watch enter hospitals or nursing homes are either not familiar with this book or do not have a copy of it with them. These individuals are well meaning and have come to comfort, but they wonder what they can offer other than the visit itself.

Here are three easy-to-implement but most potent ways of comforting and perhaps even curing the sick:

• *Visit* — That word means: Make the effort to go to the hospital, nursing institution, or home and be present in person. While you may feel uncomfortable en route, awkward while there, and frustrated returning home, nevertheless, your visit always succeeds. Being present shows you care; standing there before the sick person indicates you have not forgotten; showing concern and interest assures the ill one he or she is not alone.

Long visits are usually unnecessary or even undesirable. The fatigue of the ill person often is great and the attention span limited. Settle in enough so that the sick person senses you are not in a rush or merely fulfilling a duty. But be extremely sensitive after five to ten minutes for signs of weariness and make tentative moves to leave. Stay longer only if the confined person genuinely wishes you to stay.

Generally speaking, a half dozen ten-minute visits are better than a single hour-long stay.

• *Listen* — Allowing the sick person to talk about anything (and reflecting in your own words and by your

90

own gestures the thoughts and feelings of the one who is ill) will also always prove comforting.

This requires attention, wisdom, and discipline.

We need to pay close attention to what the ailing individual is saying to us in verbal or nonverbal ways. Often the true message is communicated underneath the words by some gesture. When a man suddenly diagnosed with leukemia tells me he would like to be around to offer his grandchildren the kind of wonderful grandfathering he received, the statement is clear enough. But his broken voice, halting sentences, and tearful eyes say much more.

This also demands the wisdom to go beneath the external words and catch the real concern. For example, when the sick one throws out heavy questions like "Why is this happening to me?" or "How could God do this?" — he or she is not usually asking you to answer those difficult, actually unanswerable queries. The interrogations instead may mirror intense inner anxiety, pain, anger, or doubt, and the ill person wants to share that interior turbulence with another who cares.

This, finally, demands discipline. We are all so wrapped up in our worlds that it is not easy to listen instead of talk. Ill individuals, particularly the critically sick, have usually lost most interest in the world outside. Rattling on about your own work, problems, or successes probably will not help the infirm person much; but sharply attentive, deeply compassionate, and accurately reflective listening will always, without exception, bring solace to the sick. You will walk away overwhelmed when the confined person says, "Thanks so much. You helped me a lot today," and you hardly made a comment but listened well.

• *Touch* — Never leave the room or bedside without in some way touching the sick person. Hold the person's hand, caress the forehead, impose hands in prayer upon the ill individual's head, moisten the lips, kiss the cheek, touch and pray over the hurting area of the body if appropriate.

Jesus and his Church have given us an example to follow in this regard. Contemporary science and pastoral practice confirm the value of that tradition. Our loving touch makes our concerned presence warmer, closer, and more effective for the sick person. It truly comforts and will help cure the ill individual spiritually, even if not physically.

9

Inner Healing

Barbara Shlemon, a registered nurse, married and the mother of five, worked as a staff nurse from 1957 through 1969. She then became involved in the healing ministry and has since lectured on the subject and worked with a healing-ministry team throughout the United States.

On one occasion Mrs. Shlemon prayed with a young woman who had suffered from constant migraine headaches for several years. That troublesome condition began immediately after she had undergone a medical abortion for a three-month pregnancy.

The youthful woman convinced herself that the abortion was justified and even bragged about the operation to others. However, her body was contradicting her rationalizing comments.

She finally agreed to seek out a priest and went to confession. The migraines completely disappeared.

The cured woman told Mrs. Shlemon afterward that it wasn't difficult to believe God could forgive her failing, but she had to fight a terrific battle learning to forgive herself.[1]

* * *

Pain, of course, is pain; and, although there are different kinds of pain, they all hurt.

We know or can try to imagine the physical pain caused by a broken bone, infected tooth, or cancerous liver. However, the inner pain brought on by one or more things — perhaps a serious moral lapse; a terrible tragedy for which we may blame (even if falsely) ourselves; a rejection by parent, spouse, friend, or colleague; a realization of our darker side — these may bother, hurt, or burden us even more than sharp bodily pains.

Moreover, as in the case — depicted at the beginning of this chapter — of the young woman suffering from migraine headaches evidently connected with having had an abortion, those inner pains may overflow into our bodily self and produce noticeable physical pain.

We have seen earlier that Jesus healed every type of disease or sickness. He was concerned about the whole person and therefore cured both physical and spiritual illnesses, both internal and external. Since we have maintained that Christ wishes to continue his healing ministry today through us, it is consequently logical to anticipate and work for the relief of inner ailments as well.

Father Francis MacNutt was one of the first Catholics to become involved in the charismatic renewal and to engage in prayer for healing. His book *Healing* contains a helpful table which summarizes four basic types of sickness (spiritual, emotional, physical, and demonic); the table also gives the cause or causes for the various types of sickness, the types of prayer and appropriate sacrament or sacramental recommended to bring about their healing, and the remedies ordinarily prescribed by modern medical doctors and their colleagues.[2]

The following is an adaptation of the above-described table:

√ Sickness of the spirit (often contributing to emotional sickness; sometimes contributing to bodily sickness). *Cause:* Personal sin. *Prayer:* Repentance. *Appropriate sacrament or sacramental:* Penance (Reconciliation). *Ordinary human remedy:* None.

√ Sickness of the emotions (often contributing to

spiritual sickness as well as physical ills). *Cause:* Original sin — that is, the person has been hurt by other people's sins. *Prayer:* Prayer for inner healing. *Appropriate sacrament or sacramental:* Penance (Reconciliation). *Ordinary human remedy:* Counseling — psychiatric and spiritual.

✓ Sickness of the body (often contributing to emotional sickness; sometimes contributing to spiritual sickness). *Cause:* Disease, accidents, psychological stress. *Prayer:* Prayer of faith for physical healing. *Appropriate sacrament or sacramental:* Anointing of the sick. *Ordinary human remedy:* Medical care.

✓ Sickness, consisting of any or all of the above, can occasionally be. . . *Cause:* Demonic in its cause. *Prayer:* Prayer of deliverance (exorcism). *Appropriate sacrament or sacramental:* Exorcism. *Ordinary human remedy:* None.

In this chapter I would like to address only troubles of the spirit or emotions (calling them inner hurts) and the cure of such burdens which I will term inner healing.

True, or Real, Guilt

The bride-to-be, whom we shall name Mary, nervously approached one of the confessionals in the church after the wedding rehearsal. She and her fiancé, having gotten "carried away" on several occasions over the past months, had taken advantage of the privileges of marriage. Mary deeply wished to confess her sin and be free of its oppressive burden before the next day's nuptials, but shame plus the fact that she knew and liked the priest-confessor complicated the matter. When her turn arrived, Mary entered the darkened enclosure, knelt, recited her lapses but, overcome by embarrassment, concealed the failings most on her mind — those premarital sexual experiences.

It was over forty years before she would ever enter

another confessional. That double dose of guilt — sexual sins and a "bad confession" — plagued her entire adult life. She sought various ways to escape the permeating and seemingly permanent pain of this unacknowledged and unexpiated wrongdoing. Mary eventually left the Church, stopped praying, and began entertaining doubts of God's existence. In addition, she suffered a minor mental and emotional breakdown.

In her early sixties, however, while watching some of the television evangelists, Mary heard words of hope which promised forgiveness. That led her gradually back to church, then to a prayer group, and finally to a priest.

The burden was gone in a few minutes. She sat before the confessor, poured from her heart the story of those four decades, and then felt his hands upon her head as he proclaimed: "God, the Father of mercies, through the death and resurrection of his Son has reconciled the world to himself and sent the Holy Spirit among us for the forgiveness of sins; through the ministry of the Church may God give you pardon and peace, and I absolve you from your sins in the name of the Father, and of the Son, ✠ and of the Holy Spirit."[3]

He gave the frail, crying, and relieved woman a reassuring hug afterward with the words, "Welcome home."

But what a waste! What a tragedy! What a needlessly burdened life! Mary lived almost all of her grown-up years under a cloud of guilt, a dark cover which could have been dissipated so easily earlier by the light of God's warm forgiveness.

Another person, similarly reconciled following a lengthy absence from grace, expressed in the following words the comparable joy of inner healing and the parallel regret that the step was so delayed: "After returning to confession for the first time in twelve years, I feel so clean, so whole, and so loved that I can only ask: Why did

I wait so long, endure so much sorrow and suffering when the Lord was there all the time?"[4]

* * *

There should be little doubt that real (that is, true) guilt can be perhaps the most crippling pain we suffer. It reaches to the core of our being; it makes us toss and turn in the middle of the night; it does not disappear like a bad dream but is there as soon as we awake in the morning; it changes our mood, interferes with our concentration, blinds us to joys, and deprives us of peace.

Real guilt, in the definition of two scholars, "is an objective state, existing when the individual has broken a law or a moral imperative."[5] It results from our sin, our failure to follow our conscience. We neglect to do what our heart tells us God commands. We follow a course of action which the divine Spirit within tells us is prohibited, or we omit a deed which the same impulse informs us is required.

We have sinned and are guilty.

This calls for repentance or a change of heart on our part and forgiveness from God for the failure.

Fortunately, the Lord's mercy is readily available, more so than we generally realize.

The Gospels contain over a dozen instances which either describe Jesus' actually forgiving the repentant sinner or teaching about the mercy of God which has no limit and lasts forever.

For example, "I tell you, there will likewise be more joy in heaven over one repentant sinner than over ninety-nine righteous people who have no need to repent" (Luke 15:7). "He said to the paralyzed man, 'My son, your sins are forgiven. . . . That you may know that the Son of Man has authority on earth to forgive sins' (he said to the paralyzed man), 'I command you: Stand up! Pick up your mat and go home' " (Mark 2:5, 10-12).

Jesus' ministry of mercy continues today. We can,

naturally, go directly to God, seek and receive forgiveness at any time. But such an immediate recourse usually lacks the deeper healing which can be found in the sacrament of penance. This ritual of reconciliation — for a variety of theological and pastoral reasons — possesses great power to bring peace.

The Church teaches that through this sacrament of penance "the faithful obtain from the mercy of God pardon for their sins against him; at the same time they are reconciled with the Church which they wounded by their sins."[6]

It also views the sacrament as a healing ritual. "Just as the wound of sin is varied and multiple in the life of individuals and of the community, so too the healing which penance provides is varied." "In order that this sacrament of healing may truly achieve its purpose among Christ's faithful, it must take root in their whole lives and move them to more fervent service of God and neighbor."[7]

Real guilt needs forgiveness from God. However, there is a false guilt sometimes equally devastating, which as such does not require divine forgiveness but instead demands natural healing, even though that cure is achieved under and perhaps more by God's hidden grace.

False Guilt

Dr. David Hilfiker graduated from the University of Minnesota Medical School and was voted by his classmates as one of the two "best clinicians." He scored well above average on his board examinations. With a spirit of generosity and dedication, he selected, after training, a remote rural area in which to work because physicians were desperately needed to relieve suffering in that section of Minnesota.

During the seven years he practiced there, his patients, partners, and peers considered him a good physician. However, he made mistakes — serious ones — that caused him severe stress, anxiety, or guilt, and which led him to leave the rural town and start off in another direction.

One of the tragic errors Dr. Hilfiker made concerned Barb and Russ Daily, friends of his, who came to Hilfiker for medical assistance when the couple discovered they were expecting a second child. Dr. Hilfiker had delivered their first infant, grew closer to them as a couple at that time, and joyfully looked forward to working with these people over the following months.

However, all the usual symptoms of a true pregnancy did not appear. He wondered about this and pondered sending Barb over a hundred miles away to Duluth for an expensive ultrasound examination. Yet Hilfiker decided not to recommend the trip, knowing that the Dailys had only a modest income and also judging that in a few weeks another local test would confirm either the pregnancy or the woman's miscarriage.

The confusing mixed signals nevertheless continued. Eventually, Dr. Hilfiker decided D & C (dilation and curettage) surgery was necessary to remove the supposedly dead embryo.

In the sixteen-bed county hospital that morning, things did not go well. Some new although slight signs indicative of a continuing vital pregnancy appeared; but in the face of the previous negative tests and his earlier diagnosis, he ignored "the information from my fingertips" and began the operation.

The surgical procedure became a nightmarish disaster. As Hilfiker proceeded, an awful panic crept over him, a growing dreadful awareness that he was aborting a living child. Subsequently, the pathologist's report confirmed his worst fears: "I had aborted a living fetus, about eleven weeks old. I had killed Barb's baby."

He continued: "During the days, the weeks, and

months after I aborted Barb's baby, my guilt and anger grew. I did discuss what had happened with my partners, with the pathologist, with obstetric specialists. Some of my mistakes were obvious: I had relied too heavily on one test; I had not been skillful in determining the size of the uterus by pelvic examination; I should have ordered the ultrasound before proceeding to the D & C. There was no way I could justify what I had done. To make matters worse, there were complications following the D & C, and Barb was unable to become pregnant again for two years.

"Although I was as honest with the Dailys as I could be, and although I told them everything they wanted to know, I never shared with them my own agony. I felt they had enough sorrow without having to bear my burden as well. I decided it was my responsibility to deal with my guilt alone. I never asked for their forgiveness."

This story is taken from an article in *Harper's* in which Dr. Hilfiker anguishes over that mistake and several others. He also mentions that physicians seemingly have no way to relieve the pain, pressure, and guilt arising from the almost unavoidable yet destructive errors which occasionally happen in the human, complex field of medicine.

"The drastic consequences of our mistakes, the repeated opportunities to make them, the uncertainty about our culpability, and the professional denial that mistakes happen all work together to create an intolerable dilemma for the physician. We see the horror of our mistakes, yet we cannot deal with their enormous emotional impact.

"Perhaps the only way to face our guilt is through confession, restitution, and absolution. Yet within the structure of modern medicine there is no place for such spiritual healing.

"Obviously, we physicians must do everything we

can to keep mistakes to a minimum. But if we are unable to deal openly with those that do occur, we will find neurotic ways to protect ourselves from the pain we feel. Little wonder that physicians are accused of playing God. Little wonder that we are defensive about our judgments, that we blame the patient or the previous physician when things go wrong, that we yell at nurses for their mistakes, that we have such high rates of alcoholism, drug addiction, and suicide."[8]

* * *

In aborting the Dailys' baby, do you think Dr. Hilfiker sinned? Would you accuse him of a moral failure? Did he violate a divine imperative, neglect to obey the Spirit's impulse, or act contrary to God's law? Simply stated, is it real guilt which burdens the man and requires the Lord's forgiveness for removal of the guilt feeling?

Or was Hilfiker's diagnosis merely a medical mistake, an unintended error of judgment, a physician's well-meaning but poorly executed attempt to help people? Again, in basic terms, is it false guilt that distresses the doctor and which needs not divine forgiveness but some type of inner healing?

Those are not really judgments for us to make. Even Dr. Hilfiker would have difficulty determining to what extent, if at all, he was morally responsible for the infant's death and therefore carries real guilt on his shoulders. Only the good Lord — who knows our sitting and our rising, who penetrates the secrets of our hearts, and who understands us better than we understand ourselves — can accurately assess the situation.

The case of Dr. Hilfiker, nevertheless, does illustrate the complexity behind the reality of guilt and the ambiguity in the word's meaning. It also underscores the possibility of false guilt unnecessarily overwhelming an individual and depriving that person of peace.

101

Such false guilt can develop particularly as a result of these tendencies, circumstances, or situations:

• *Making moral molehills into mortal-sin mountains.* Persons with this tendency judge that minor character flaws or venial sins are major, mortal failures which break our friendship with God. They exaggerate the degree of evil present and allow that distortion to rob them of serenity, or peace.

• *Never letting go of forgiven sins.* We need always to stand before God as sinners in need of grace and salvation. We also can benefit from an awareness of past misdeeds — such a consciousness may enhance a healthy humility and sharpen our sensitivity in dealing with the human frailty of others. But worrying about whether sins have actually been forgiven, becoming obsessed with past misdeeds, and not allowing God's mercy previously bestowed in confession to liberate us from those faults — these things can and do cripple the person.

• *Blaming ourselves for events beyond our control or responsibility.* This inaccurate self-blame and the false guilt which flows from it often revolve around: (1) Accidents. A classmate of mine, one year out of high school, was driving home in the early summer twilight, when a young child dashed out from the grassy, country roadside into the path of her car. The youngster died instantly. My friend had to deal with heavy guilt feelings for years even though she was totally free of blame for the tragic accident. (2) Parents whose children have failed in some way. They question and blame themselves when children develop an addiction for drugs or alcohol, drop out of school, become pregnant outside of marriage, run afoul of the law, cease attending church, or otherwise falter and fail to follow the course pointed out by Mom and Dad. Mothers and fathers subsequently torture themselves with self-doubts and experience deep guilt even though objective outsiders would testify that their parenting was informed and conscientious. (3) Children in their relationship with aging or infirm parents. They wrestle with guilt about not visiting parents often enough, placing feeble ones in nursing homes, and being absent at the moment of death. (4) Suicides. Survivors of suicide victims, looking back, often castigate themselves for their failure to detect suicidal signs or even see in their own actions possible causes for the tragic deed. One young widow, absolutely distraught over her husband's suicide, still wept profusely one month later and kept exclaiming, "I feel so guilty." In that context, the woman blew up normal marital disagreements beyond all proportion and judged them to be the motivation for her spouse's self-destructive tendencies and ultimate act.[9]

Those afflicted with false guilt require inner healing more than forgiveness. God's grace, some of the steps to be sketched subsequently in this chapter, and perhaps professional therapy are the vehicles which can bring that about.

Past Hurts and Bad Memories

When Sam was a young boy his father often beat him up and his mother frequently put him down. It seemed to them he never did do anything right and it seemed to him he never could do anything right.

As this failure-ridden and guilt-burdened lad entered his teens, he found a refuge from such oppressive feelings. At the age of sixteen, Sam discovered temporary relief in alcohol and began to anesthetize himself regularly with liquor. This heavy drinking to deaden his inner pain continued for the next twenty-six years.

He functioned well enough to maintain a good job as an artistic designer in the advertising field. Sam also married but only out of sheer loneliness. Predictably, that union lasted only three or four years. There were no children from the marriage, partially because in his

103

drunken stupor the man could barely function sexually.

The alcohol blotted out for a few moments his intense anxieties about failure and guilt, but the next morning they resurfaced and with them renewed bouts of self-loathing. That recurrence in turn simply pushed him out the door and into a bar.

One day he parked illegally before a package store and left his car for the building to purchase a few quarts of liquor. An automobile swerved past him and the driver angrily shouted, "You can't park there!"

This remark stunned Sam. At forty-two he had recently begun to reflect on his pathetic condition. The interior pain was becoming so great and the hurts so deep that he no longer felt able to endure them. The sarcastic comment yelled from a speeding auto suddenly put his sad existence into focus. Sam recognized that death would soon overtake him unless he took some drastic steps.

The middle-aged man attended an AA (Alcoholics Anonymous) meeting and after the first session started changing his ways.

Following two years of sobriety, Sam's head had cleared a bit and he came to recognize that there were some hidden causes behind his drinking. That led him to a professional counselor who helped Sam recognize a few of the neuroses, the unconscious impulses, the past hurts, and bad memories which deprived him of peace and ultimately drove him to seek escape in the bottle.

Sam is now a man of profound serenity. He has actually wept with joy on occasions when a never-before-experienced inner calm overwhelmed him. He spends twenty minutes a day in prayer, stops in church often, and possesses a deep intellectual as well as an almost tangible awareness of being loved by God.

Those troublesome voices from earlier years sometimes surface and create urges within him again to seek solace in alcohol. Sam, however, more clearly understands the compulsions and is better able to deal with them.

Sam considers himself healed by the grace of God which has worked through its direct yet hidden influences upon his own heart, through the voice of an annoyed motorist, through the support of the AA program, and through the wise counseling of a gentle therapist.

* * *

One does not have to look hard or listen long to discover how many Sams there are in today's world, people with crippling bad memories of conscious or unconscious hurts.

Jesuit Father Robert Faricy teaches theology in Rome, is actively involved with the healing ministry, and in his book *Praying for Inner Healing* describes some of those inner wounds.

Noting that physical, psychological, and spiritual hurts and healings interact and overlap, Father Faricy observes, "All of us, at least sometimes, have experienced inner suffering, or conflicts, or strong and unreasonable anger or fear or sadness."[10]

The Jesuit professor, in analyzing the causes behind these wounds, tells us: "We know from psychology and psychiatry that much of what needs to be healed in us is buried beneath the level of consciousness. Interior suffering or stress or sadness frequently results from root problems or hurts or wounds or conflicts that are not conscious, that we are not aware of. We see only the tips of the icebergs that need to be melted. It is not necessary to know with precision what needs healing, although it helps. We can pray to be healed, interiorly, in our emotions, insofar as we are aware that we need healing, and then we can let the Lord take it from there and guide us to what we should do or pray for next.

"Where do these — mostly unconscious — hurts

come from? They come from the very beginning of our existence, from our earliest years, from our childhood and growing up, from the whole process of living. Some of them are so early and so deeply repressed that we can never get at them; but Our Lord sees them all and can heal them all. Many interior wounds, both conscious and buried, result from poor or inadequate home life in childhood, from negative aspects of school life, from setbacks in childhood or in later life. In many cases, things have been done to people which ought never to have been done, a lot of suffering was caused, and healing is needed."[11]

These hurts can upset our lives and interfere with the proper functioning of our faculties.

For example, our affective life may be so disturbed that we have a relative incapacity to love or to receive the love of others, a fearfulness, timidity, or shyness that severely limits communication with others, or a general depression that almost totally immobilizes us.

In addition, these wounds may result in habits or tendencies — suspiciousness, selfishness, undesirable behavior — which deprive us of peace and complicate our relationship with God.

Father Faricy offers a few specific illustrations of memories which, like those of Sam, need healing: "Childhood memories of an overstrict father or a possessive mother, or of an alcoholic or otherwise ill parent, or of poverty, or loneliness, or fear of a certain teacher, or shame at being too fat, or of an accident or physical abuse or a thousand other things. These trouble-causing memories will be found to contain one or more of the four typical reactions to stress: anger (or bitterness or resentment), fear (or withdrawal), anxiety, or guilt feelings."[12]

Franciscan Father Michael Scanlan, a college president who holds a Harvard law degree, also has been active in the healing ministry. His paperback, titled *Inner*

Healing, cites various hurts afflicting people and healings which resulted from prayer: "We have prayed for women who hated men, men who rebelled against all authority figures in their life, men and women who were convinced they were unlovable and acted that way, men and women who couldn't place trust in anyone else, alcoholics, dope addicts, schizophrenics, those whose lives were substantially impaired by fears of darkness, being alone, failure, sex, and most commonly those with dominating feelings of guilt and inferiority. In every case where there was a series of contacts there has been improvement. In each category mentioned there has been a person substantially or fully healed as best we can determine.

"We refer here to our experience of healings and not miracles. We do not have demonstrable evidence that the only explanation for the healing was the direct action of God. What we have are beautiful striking experiences in which we prayed for the Lord's action, we believed in the Lord's presence and we observed significant improvement that seemed directly related to the Lord's power. We have prayed for two married women who underwent extensive psychiatric treatment to the point where the various doctors told them they could give no hope for improvement. Both had to cease any employment and were at the point of being committed to a mental institution. After prayer both improved significantly and now are working and living in happier homes . . . [although the two] still are suffering from some anxiety."[13]

Shortly we will outline a few practical steps for this kind of prayer for inner healing.

Our Darker Side

In a popular movie, the star plays the role of a single parent with two children who works as a detective in New Orleans stalking a deranged murderer of prostitutes.

The criminal has a preference for bizarre, destructive sexual behavior; but as the story unfolds, the detective realizes he has within himself some of those same frightening tendencies. Trying to track down the killer, he consults a female psychologist for some insights about the man and those deviant inclinations.

She explains to the detective that we all have this darker side of ourselves. Some people, like the murderer, act out these negative desires; others identify and learn how to control them; while still others ignore or may seek to repress those inner undesirable impulses.

The detective eventually captures the killer; but, moreover, he breaks the grip these fears of his darker side had upon him and thereby allows himself to be loved in a genuine way by another.

* * *

The movie communicates this truth about our darker side with such dramatic force that we might find the explicitness particularly offensive or the tale a mere fantasy. Nevertheless, any honest personal reflection will reveal past actions of our own which make us wince now, or expose certain current tendencies toward unbecoming behavior within us against which we struggle.

Such recognition should not surprise us. St. Paul wrote centuries ago about this tension or war within him as well as within us: "I cannot even understand my own actions. I do not do what I want to do but what I hate. When I act against my own will, by that very fact I agree that the law is good. This indicates that it is not I who do it but sin which resides in me. I know that no good dwells in me, that is, in my flesh; the desire to do right is there but not the power. What happens is that I do, not the good I will to do, but the evil I do not intend. But if I do what is against my will, it is not I who do it, but sin which dwells in me. This means that even though I want to do what is right, a law that leads to wrongdoing is always ready at hand. My inner self agrees with the law of God, but I see in my body's members another law at war with the law of my mind; this makes me the prisoner of the law of sin in my members. What a wretched man I am! Who can free me from this body under the power of death? All praise to God, through Jesus Christ our Lord! So with my mind I serve the law of God but with my flesh the law of sin" (Romans 7:15-25).

To accept that part of myself likewise requires inner healing. We will now suggest some ways to seek this remedy and to be healed of guilt, past hurts, bad memories, and our darker side.

Steps for Inner Healing

The late Archbishop Fulton J. Sheen mentioned in his autobiography that if he were to begin his electronic ministry today, he would reverse the approach taken decades ago. The prelate in his preaching then started with the order of the universe around us and from that led hearers to the God who is the source of such beauty and harmony. Today he would begin with the disorder inside us and move from there to the God who heals and frees us from such interior turmoil.[14]

Dr. Robert Schuller, the "Hour of Power" television evangelist and Crystal Cathedral founder, would agree. He believes that an unfulfilled need for self-esteem motivates every human action today. People in general — according to him — possess poor self-images, wish to develop better ones, and try various means to accomplish that goal. Unfortunately, some of the ways attempted to achieve an enhanced self-concept move in false directions and aggravate rather than alleviate the problem. Schuller proposes "The Lord's Prayer: His Healing Way" as the solution to the modern search for self-esteem.[15]

Father Jim McManus, a Redemptorist priest from

Scotland who has been active for many years in the healing and renewal ministries, likewise might concur with Archbishop Sheen and Dr. Schuller. His recent book, *The Healing Power of the Sacraments,* describes in theory and practice prayer's power to heal as well as the potential for healing in the sacraments of reconciliation, anointing of the sick, and the Eucharist. He also stresses the need to cure our wounded self-images through prayer and the sacraments.

The Redemptorist argues that because of the sinful or evil condition of the world around us (our doing, not God's) we are wounded in our self-esteem or self-image, our relationships, and our memories. The inner healing needed to cure those wounds he consequently defines in these words: "Inner healing is an experience of the healing love of God in which the person realizes that he or she is lovable (healing of the self-image), or capable of loving and forgiving someone (healing of relationships), or able to gratefully accept some past event (healing of memories)."[16]

I wish here to summarize and make my own Father McManus's suggestions and Father Faricy's recommendations for inner healing through prayer.

• *Accept with wonder, praise, and thanks the fact that we are special in the sight of God.* Both the Hebrew Scriptures (Old Testament) and the New Testament give ample testimony about our dignity and specialness. The Book of Psalms reminds us that we have been made "little less than the angels," crowned with glory and honor and given "rule over the works of your hands" (Psalm 8:6-7).

Jesus, while promising his followers protection in the face of persecution, emphasized our uniqueness before God. " 'Are not five sparrows sold for a few pennies? Yet not one of them is neglected by God. In very truth, even the hairs of your head are counted! Fear nothing, then.

110

You are worth more than a flock of sparrows' " (Luke 12:6-7).

Inspired words like these, allowed to sink into the depths of our hearts, will lead us to develop an attitude of gratitude over the wonder of our being. At Mass, for example, the priest — in our behalf — expresses the notion during the second eucharistic prayer: "We thank you for counting us worthy to stand in your presence and serve you."

Father McManus would have us reflect on this truth regularly, even daily, in our personal prayer as well — especially if we are struggling with a bad time or a poor self-image. He tells us that "when we feel bad about something," "instead of yielding to feelings of self-destruction and self-pity" we should simply pray: "I thank you for my being. I praise you that I am precious to you."

He goes on to say: "People who spend five minutes in the morning praising God for the wonder of their being will have no problem in coping with attacks on their self-image during the day. I always ask those who are suffering from a poor self-image to spend at least five minutes hearing the word that they are precious to God and responding to it with praise and thanks. So many people don't feel precious to God or to anyone else! They are depressed with sadness and loneliness; they fear that nobody will ever love them. They feel like this because they do not love themselves. Self-acceptance, true self-love, is a grace given to us when we accept God's word about ourselves."[17]

• *Acknowledge with the same wonder, praise, and thanks the fact that others — including, even particularly, those who have hurt us — are special in God's sight.* When people injure us in some big or small way we usually experience a resentment which can linger or fester and harden our hearts. It often creates a distance and alienation between us. It deprives us of peace and may lead to other negative results.

Father McManus again tells us how prayer for inner healing can help: "We bring before the Lord the people with whom we share our lives, and we praise God that they too are precious in his sight. It is very important for us to bring before the Lord in this way anyone who is causing us some problem. It is important to mention each person by name, in the presence of God, and accept the person as God's precious creation. If someone has upset us, it will be difficult for us to see that person in a good light. Hence the need to see him or her in the light of the word of God. We may be sad and depressed because someone has offended us, and we can no longer relate to that person. We feel hurt and let down. When we think of the person all those hurt feelings begin to come up. The temptation, then, is to repress the feelings, to pretend that they are not there. Instead of repressing the hurt feelings, we should bring them into the presence of God and praise God for the person who hurt our feelings. As we praise God for that person, as we acknowledge that that person is precious to God, our hurt feelings begin to experience healing. We may be angry, but instead of letting the anger become aggressive or abusive, we admit that we are angry and thank God for those with whom we are angry. It is impossible to say, 'Lord, I bless you for Peter, who has hurt me,' and continue to hold on to resentment against him."[18]

• *Recognize with joy and gratitude all the good that God does in our lives and in the lives of others.* Reflectively praying in this manner counteracts our tendency to maximize our mistakes and misfortunes. It also serves as an effective antidote to jealous thoughts or feelings about others. Finally, it helps overcome that inclination to spread pejorative gossip, criticize our neighbor, or rejoice over someone's failures.

McManus makes these comments about that type of acknowledging prayer and urges us to take a few moments every morning to recognize what God is doing in our lives and the lives of others: "If we don't praise God for what he is doing in others, we will become jealous of them, and their successes will begin to deprive us of our peace. The sure sign of jealousy is the inability to acknowledge that someone has done a good job. This prayer of acknowledgment is the best way to deal with jealousy. It is impossible to remain jealous while acknowledging the good things God is doing in another person. As we acknowledge what God is doing in another, our image of that person is transformed. We begin to see him or her as a collaborator with God. If the person has hurt us in any way, this prayer of acknowledgment brings a deep and lasting healing."[19]

• *Repent, with faith in God's limitless love and forgiveness.* A healthy Christian spirituality integrates a clear perception of our own wounded, limited, sinful state with an awareness of God's far greater love, compassion, and saving power. A physician can do no good unless a patient seeks help and reveals the symptoms of sickness. The Divine Physician, likewise, awaits our call.

Father Faricy details what that type of repentance coupled with faith means: "This includes the renunciation of sin and a conversion, a turning towards God in humility to accept his mercy and forgiving love. It helps to remember that the Lord came to save not the just but sinners, and that my very sinfulness attracts his loving compassion, that the dark side of myself that I find hard to accept he accepts totally and lovingly, and that my very weakness is the opening in me to him and to his saving strength which is made perfect in my weakness.

"I want to accept the Lord's forgiveness and to let him heal me."[20]

• *Forgive those who have hurt us.* This is the

113

simple but difficult price tag God has attached to divine forgiveness. Unless we forgive others, we cannot expect the Lord's forgiveness. "Forgive us our trespasses as we forgive those who trespass against us" is our daily prayer and the one Jesus taught us. Christ also warned, " 'If you forgive the faults of others, your heavenly Father will forgive you yours. If you do not forgive others, neither will your Father forgive you' " (Matthew 6:14-15).

Faricy puts the matter this way: "Failure to forgive other persons the pain and the hurt that they have caused me can block me, can close me to the healing power of Jesus. The resentment or the anger that I feel towards a person who has hurt me can act as a hard shell around the inner wound that that person caused."[21]

Acknowledging and recognizing in prayer by name the specialness of others and what God is doing through them is an effective tool to soften our hearts and enable us to forgive those who have hurt us.

• *Forgive ourselves.* The young woman at the start of this chapter said it wasn't difficult to believe that God could forgive her failing, but she had to fight a terrific battle learning to forgive herself.

That self-forgiveness is an ongoing struggle, one that surfaces every now and then, often over the same or similar incident with the regrets which we thought had been put to rest.

Faricy stresses the importance of this step in inner healing: "I need to accept Jesus' and the Father's total and unconditional acceptance of me; accepting God's acceptance of me, I can accept myself. Our Lord loves me not in spite of the dark side of myself but partly because of it; he came to save not the just but sinners, and my sinfulness attracts his loving compassion."[22]

• *Forgive God.* God clearly has neither sinned nor hurt us. But with our human limitations we may judge that to be the case and harbor ill feelings toward the Lord.

Jesuit Father Faricy deals with this issue as well: "Sometimes we need to forgive God. Obviously, there is no fault at all in God. Nevertheless, I might feel, in a vague way, some resentment against God for my own limitations or failures, for illness or an accident, for the death of someone I love, or for circumstances of my life. God wants me to forgive him, so that I can get over my resentment, accept his love better, and be healed."[23]

Oil, Bread, Wine, and the Forces of Evil

To conclude this lengthy chapter on inner healing, I would like to touch briefly upon several points connected with the topic.

• The use of *nonsacramental oil* in prayer for healing. The holy water with which Roman Catholics bless themselves at the entrance to the church and which is used to bless people or objects on other occasions is a reminder of the sacramental water used in baptism. In parallel fashion, a growing number of people today have begun to employ a blessed oil similar to the sacramental oil applied to the body during the ritual for anointing of the sick when they pray for those who are in any way ill or hurting.

The older Roman Ritual contains a blessing for such oil immediately after the blessing of lard and immediately before the blessing of oats. This prayer of blessing (limited to a bishop or priest) as well as the rubrical directions do not restrict its use to the clergy. In fact the text almost presumes lay persons will be the main people employing this oil: "Grant, we pray, that those who will use this oil, which we are blessing in your name, may be delivered from all suffering, all infirmity, and all the wiles of the enemy. . . ."[24]

Parish leaders need to explain the oil's value, indicate its difference from the oil in the sacrament of anointing, and show how in practice the oil can be applied during prayer for healing.

• The *Holy Eucharist*: the sun, the center, and the summit of the Church and its worship. The Vatican Council Fathers wrote that "from the liturgy, therefore, and especially from the Eucharist, grace is poured forth upon us as from a fountain, . . ."[25]

It should not be a surprise, consequently, to note in the liturgical texts for Mass frequent references to healing. We already have mentioned the response before communion. Here are a few others: (1) The penitential rite: "You were sent to heal the contrite." (2) Following the Our Father: "Deliver us, Lord, from every evil, and grant us peace in our day. In your mercy keep us free from sin and protect us from all anxiety. . . ." (3) Prayer before communion: Let your body and blood "not bring me condemnation, but health in mind and body." (4) While cleansing the vessels: May these gifts "bring me healing and strength, now and forever." (5) First eucharistic prayer of reconciliation: "By the power of your Holy Spirit, make them one body, healed of all division." (6) Prayer after communion, Monday, first week of Lent: "Lord, through this sacrament may we rejoice in your healing power and experience your saving love in mind and body."

The Forces of Evil

There is great controversy today about both the forces of evil around us and the existence of a personal devil, usually referred to as Satan or the Evil One. Moreover, a parallel debate rages about the prayer of deliverance and formal exorcisms for people whose afflictions seem caused at least in part by some type of demonic influence.

The Church has a long tradition which maintains the

reality of such diabolic forces, and its ritual book actually provides a formal exorcism for use in cases of demonic possession, obsession, or similar circumstances.

Nevertheless, because of the obvious complexity and inherent dangers in this area, only those with wisdom and experience should attempt exorcisms or prayers of deliverance.

MacNutt deals with these issues in a chapter of his book entitled *Healing*.[26]

Some years ago a fanatic dealt several damaging blows to Michelangelo's Pietà located in an alcove at the right of the entrance to St. Peter's Basilica in Rome.

When the world's best sculptors arrived in Italy to restore the masterpiece, they did not immediately begin to work on the statue. Instead, they spent months studying the work of art before them trying to capture in their minds what Michelangelo had originally created. After they had a picture of this in their minds, the artists went to work restoring the statue's pristine beauty.[27]

With us, God is like one of those artists. The beauty we possessed upon first entering the world has been disfigured by our own failures and the harmful acts of others. However, the Lord immediately starts to refashion us just as soon as we disfigure ourselves or suffer some disfigurement from others. God wishes to restore our original beauty, to heal our wounds, and to cure our brokenness.

10

Preparing for
the Journey

Ann George spent her last fifteen days on earth at home.

She had gone temporarily to a hospital when pain caused by cancer grew unbearable. However, drugs were able to reduce that agony, and the thirty-eight-year-old wife and mother of two preferred being in her own house and in her own bed rather than in a hospital room.

The parish priest came to the home daily with holy communion under the form of viaticum for this woman whose thin body and furrowed brow reflected the pain and worry connected with her condition.

In the beginning he would place the standard-size consecrated host on her hand. But soon her weakened condition required that she receive it directly upon the tongue. Gradually he had to reduce the size of the particle because of Ann's difficulty with swallowing. Eventually, her condition required him to take a spoonful of water, drop the small piece of eucharistic bread into it, and help her communicate by actually spoon-feeding her.

Each time, however, besides the words "the Body of Christ," he added the formula proper to viaticum: "May the Lord Jesus Christ protect you and lead you to eternal life."

On one occasion, with Ann's husband and two children (ages eleven and eight) present, the priest invited them to touch their spouse and mother during the concluding blessing. As they did so, she turned and gave them all a weak but magnificent smile which seemed to say, "I love you and I know you love me."

The last time this woman received viaticum her pastor recited the following prayer after communion:

God of peace,
you offer eternal healing to those who believe in you;
you have refreshed your servant Ann,
with food and drink from heaven:
lead her safely into the kingdom of light.[1]

Two days later Ann closed her eyes and began her journey into that kingdom of light and eternal life.

Viaticum

Viaticum is more truly today the Church's liturgical rite for those who are dying. The word means, literally, "(food) with you on the way." In the introduction to this ritual the text states: "The celebration of the eucharist as viaticum, food for the passage through death to eternal life, is the sacrament proper to the dying Christian. It is the completion and crown of the Christian life on this earth, signifying that the Christian follows the Lord to eternal glory and the banquet of the heavenly kingdom."[2]

Here are several practical points stressed by the ritual in connection with viaticum:

• The *purpose* of viaticum and the other rites in Part II of the ritual book is "to comfort and strengthen a dying Christian in the passage from this life. The ministry to the dying places emphasis on trust in the Lord's promise of eternal life rather than on the struggle against illness which is characteristic of the pastoral care of the sick."[3]

• The *entire Christian community,* not simply the clergy or the family, has a duty to care for the dying person. "The Christian community has a continuing responsibility to pray for and with the person who is dying. Through its sacramental ministry to the dying the community helps Christians to embrace death in mysterious union with the crucified and risen Lord, who awaits them in the fullness of life."[4]

• Those *who have already died* are not normally anointed unless there is a chance life remains within them. "A priest is not to administer the sacrament of anointing. Instead, he should pray for the dead person, using prayers such as those which appear in this chapter. He may find it necessary to explain to the family of the person who is dead that sacraments are celebrated for the living, not for the dead, and that the dead are effectively helped by the prayers of the living."[5]

• "Whenever it is possible, the dying Christian should be able to receive *viaticum within Mass*. In this way he or she shares fully, during the final moments of this life, in the eucharistic sacrifice, which proclaims the Lord's own passing through death to life. However, circumstances, such as confinement to a hospital ward or the very emergency which makes death imminent, may frequently make the complete eucharistic celebration impossible. In this case, the rite for viaticum outside Mass is appropriate."[6]

• "A distinctive feature of the celebration of viaticum, whether within or outside Mass, is the *renewal of the baptismal profession of faith* by the dying person. This occurs after the homily and replaces the usual form of the profession of faith. Through the baptismal profession at the end of earthly life, the one who is dying uses the language of his or her initial commitment, which is renewed each Easter and on other occasions in the Christian life. In the context of viaticum, it is a renewal and fulfillment of initiation into the Christian mysteries, baptism leading to the eucharist."[7]

• "The rites for viaticum within and outside Mass may include the *sign of peace*. The minister and all who are present embrace the dying Christian. In this and in other parts of the celebration the sense of leave-taking need not be concealed or denied, but the joy of Christian hope, which is the comfort and strength of the one near death, should also be evident."[8]

• The dying person and all who are present may receive *communion under both kinds*. The sign of communion is more complete when received in this manner because it expresses more fully and clearly the nature of the eucharist as a meal, one which prepares all who take part in it for the heavenly banquet.

"The sick who are unable to receive under the form of bread may receive under the form of wine alone."[9]

• "It often happens that a person who has received the eucharist as *viaticum* lingers in a grave condition or at the point of death for a period of days or longer. In these circumstances he or she should be given the opportunity to receive the eucharist as viaticum on successive days, *frequently if not daily*."[10]

In the rite of viaticum itself, there are appropriate prayers, readings, and blessings which underscore the notion of preparing the dying for the journey to eternity. For example, an alternative acclamation immediately before communion reads, "Jesus Christ is the food for our journey; he calls us to the heavenly table."[11]

Commendation of the Dying

Kenneth Herbert joined the Catholic Church several months before his death. As a commercial house painter throughout most of his life, he soon discovered that this profession had ruined his lungs, and the resulting emphysema normally made it difficult for him to speak above a whisper.

A parish priest called upon Kenneth at the local hospital late one evening and offered to pray with him. After fulfilling Kenneth's request for the "green pastures prayer" (Psalm 23, "The Good Shepherd"), the pastor knelt down by the side of the bed and whispered into Kenneth's ear short biblical texts provided in the "Commendation of the Dying" section of the ritual, adhering to its rubrical directions: "The prayers are best said in a slow, quiet voice, alternating with periods of silence. If possible, the minister says one or more of the brief prayer formulas with the dying person. These may be softly repeated two or three times."[12]

As this priest spoke the first phrase, "Who can separate us from the love of Christ?" (Romans 8:35), Kenneth Herbert moved his head from side to side. In effect he was saying, "Nothing can or will separate me from the love of Christ."

The pastor went on. When he recited, "We shall see God as he really is" (1 John 3:2), Kenneth began to say something with his failing voice, made nearly inaudible because of emphysema.

The priest stood up, bent over Kenneth's mouth to catch his words, and heard, "How beautiful it will be to kneel in the presence of God and see God as he really is."

* * *

Through viaticum the dying person becomes united with Christ in his passage out of this world to the Father. Through the prayers for the commendation of the dying, the Church helps to sustain that union until it is brought to fulfillment after death.[13]

These texts include appropriate prayers, litanies, aspirations, psalms, and biblical readings which "are intended to help the dying person, if still conscious, to face the natural human anxiety about death by imitating Christ in his patient suffering and dying. The Christian will be helped to surmount his or her fear in the hope of heavenly life and resurrection through the power of

Christ, who destroyed the power of death by his own dying.

"Even if the dying person is not conscious, those who are present will draw consolation from these prayers and come to a better understanding of the paschal character of Christian death. This may be visibly expressed by making the sign of the cross on the forehead of the dying person, who was first signed with the cross at baptism."[14]

All those things that were said about comforting the sick in Chapter 8 — to visit, listen, and touch — apply with special force in the case of those who are dying. However, here are some additional suggestions to make those visitations effective and satisfying:

• *Come to grips with your own eventual death.* I recently visited with a middle-aged business executive on a Sunday night flight to Chicago's O'Hare airport. Two tragedies had struck over the past months — an accident seriously injuring a favorite next-door neighbor and an advanced cancer rapidly consuming his young brother-in-law. My companion openly admitted his lifelong fear and reluctance even to enter any hospital. He also perceives now that this antipathy stems from a failure to understand, come to grips with, and accept the reality of his own inevitable demise.

Those who are dying will swiftly intuit our feelings about death — whether it be fear, denial, anger, or acceptance. Consequently, visitors to critically ill individuals need to reflect personally about this natural fact of life, our certain deaths — and seek to be at least realistic about, if not comfortable with, it.

• *Understand the common feelings and attitudes experienced by dying people.* Dr. Elisabeth Kübler-Ross, a psychiatrist who directs the Family Service and Mental Health Center of South Cook County in Chicago, wrote a book in 1969 called *On Death and*

Dying.[15] It has since become a classic reference work on the subject.

She discovered that dying patients generally pass through or experience certain common stages, attitudes, or feelings during their illness: denial, anger, bargaining, depression or sadness, and acceptance.

An awareness of these stages, and of ways to respond when they occur, obviously can be quite beneficial for those attending or visiting the infirm.

It should be noted that these different feelings, moods, attitudes, or reactions often — in fact, usually — occur also among members of the sick person's family and those close to the critically ill patient.

One must observe at the outset that these stages are neither chronological nor static, nor always present. Patients do not necessarily move from the first through each to the last. They may likewise go back and forth, in and out of different stages. Finally, desperately sick patients may skip one stage or another, or not even reach the final attitude, which is acceptance.

Sometimes merely talking about these stages in a theoretical way to a seriously sick person without probing or accusation can touch those inner feelings and ease or heal them.

The loving Christian who spends many hours and makes frequent visits by the bedside will find that an awareness of these stages — no matter how little the awareness may be — helps greatly in responding to the shifting and various moods of the critically ill. It will similarly assist the caring healthy individual who senses he or she has been experiencing or working through some or all of the same stages.

Michael Johnson had sold his business and invested the entire proceeds from that sale into a new, promising venture five years earlier. This daring but reasonable and potentially profitable step was about to become productive and successful when he developed severe back problems. Diagnosis indicated the presence of a serious, inoperable cancer which his doctors said would probably claim his life in a relatively short period of time.

I visited Michael in the hospital and chatted with him for a bit, then inquired, "Mike, when people are seriously ill they often go through some common feelings or definite stages. Would you be interested in hearing about them?"

He gave an affirmative nod and I then proceeded to summarize in ten minutes those five stages and explain some practical applications which flow from them.

Michael wept. After a few moments he remarked, "I have been through all of them."

Simply to hear someone state in words what he had been painfully but secretly feeling inside, to know these are normal stages, to understand that it is natural, for example to become angry with others and God — these things were most helpful for this afflicted fellow.

• *Remember that the sense of hearing usually is the last faculty to lose its power.* There is both a positive and a negative implication to that truth.

Negatively, we should be careful about our conversations around the bedside of a dying person, even if that individual is unconscious, seemingly unable to speak, understand, or communicate. He or she may well grasp more than we judge. Our remarks, therefore, should be comments that will be encouraging and constructive, not destructive and discouraging.

Positively, we should make efforts frequently to speak into the ear of the dying person words of love and faith, including the type of biblical phrases described in connection with the hospital visit to Kenneth Herbert at the start of this chapter.

Frances Clancy had uttered nothing for two days but repeated "Ahs" from her hospital bed when the parish

125

priest stopped to visit. He bent over next to her ear and whispered that it was Father N. coming to be with her. She said, "Father," then resumed the "Ahs" until she died a day later.

We never know what is being heard and understood at those moments.

In an earlier book, *Together by Your Side*, I outlined those stages surrounding death with their practical impact and included prayers like the short texts for the "Commendation of the Dying" from the ritual. It was and continues to be my hope that caring people, through this manual, would thus more easily and effectively be able to comfort their loved ones who are near death.[16]

• *Trace the sign of the cross frequently upon the dying person's forehead.* The Church in its practical suggestions for those who assist dying sister or brother Christians stresses the need to proclaim and explain the paschal (that is, Easter) character of death. That means Christ — by his own suffering, dying, and rising — destroyed our death and gave us the hope of heavenly life and resurrection. To paraphrase St. Paul: "If we die with the Lord, we shall also rise with him" (see 1 Thessalonians 4:16-17).

As we have seen above, this paschal mystery of Christian death "may be visibly expressed by making the sign of the cross on the forehead of the dying person, who was first signed with the cross of baptism."

In the revised baptismal liturgy, we welcome the new Christian to our Church family by tracing a sign of the cross on the forehead. As the Christian prepares to leave this life and religious family, we repeat the gesture. Thus, on every occasion that we step out of the dying person's room for a period of time, we should make a silent cross upon the loved one's brow.

• *Touch or hold the dying person, especially at the last moments of life.* Those who are seriously ill

126

through sickness, accident, or old age generally experience the pain of isolation and desolation.

Elderly people particularly may feel desolate because many or most of their friends have died. Grace Casey — whom we talked about in Chapter 8 of this book — knows that desolation well; and she knows it well because all of her card-playing partners have left this earth for the world to come.

Critically ill individuals also tend to feel isolated because they in fact usually are cut off from the daily flow of society by being placed in nursing institutions and intensive-care units or confined at home.

This double burden of desolation and isolation can make a person feel alone or lonely and heightens the importance of a visitor or health-care personnel communicating presence by touch.

Especially as the last moments arrive, those gathered together at the dying person's side are encouraged to touch the patient, grasp his or her hand, caress the forehead, even hold the departing Christian in one's arms.

An infant is held lovingly when it enters the world and our Christian community. Fittingly, years later, as a dying believer, the grown-up child would also be held lovingly — when he or she leaves God's family on earth for a permanent home in heaven.

When Christiane Brusselmans, the internationally known religious educator, was caring for her seriously ill father at home, his physician stopped by the house one day, visited with the ailing man, and, before leaving, picked him up and held him in his arms.

Upon his departure, the doctor turned to Ms. Brusselmans and suggested, even commanded, "Christiane, when the time comes for your father to go, just pick him up and hold him. Hold him — so he will not be alone when he leaves this world."

I understand that in those ultimate moments the person at the side of the dying individual — and holding the individual — is perceived by the dying one as the one he or she would want there. That perception may also change from minute to minute.

For example, when my mother finally died in the arms of my stepfather after a long and difficult bout with cancer, her three children were not physically present. But on that occasion he was to be simultaneously himself, me, my brother, my sister, and all those others close and dear to her.

Who is present is not quite as important as making sure that someone is by the dying person's side throughout those final hours. This can be helpful and consoling to concerned relatives. Instead of the entire family maintaining an exhaustive vigil for days during the last moments, they might do well to work out a schedule so that one member is constantly on hand and ministering in the ways described above. The others could easily be summoned when death appears imminent; but should they not make it and not be present in an actual physical manner, their peace of mind could be assured knowing that someone who cares was constantly by the loved one's side to the very end.

I have a dream, or vision, that every Catholic parish eventually will have a corps of persons comfortable with the thought of their own deaths, knowledgeable about the stages of dying, aware of the importance of listening and touching, familiar with the Church's special prayers for the dying, and willing to spend time by the bedside of a critically ill person. With such a group of volunteers we could then hope that no Catholic, no Christian, no human being would ever die alone.

The Church points out that "immediately after death has occurred, all may kneel while one of those present leads the prayers'' available after death for the family and friends.[17] This is one of those texts:

Almighty and eternal God,
hear our prayers for your son/daughter N.,
whom you have called from this life to yourself.

Grant him/her light, happiness, and peace.
Let him/her pass in safety through the gates of death,
and live for ever with all your saints
in the light you promised to Abraham
and to all his descendants in faith.

Guard him/her from all harm
and on that great day of resurrection and reward
raise him/her up with all your saints.
Pardon his/her sins
and give him/her eternal life in your kingdom.[18]

As the last preparation for the deceased's journey to eternity, the minister may bless the person, trace a cross on the forehead, and sprinkle the body with holy water.[19] As a new Christian, this individual was held, blessed, signed with a cross, and washed in the waters of baptism. Now, fittingly, the same person leaves us held, blessed, signed with a cross, and sprinkled with water which reminds us of baptism, that sacrament which opens for us the doors to everlasting life.

11

Comfort for
Those Who Mourn

When Sam Joseph approached death, he grew apprehensive and pleaded with his wife and thirty-year-old daughter not to leave him. They did not; they remained by his bedside in the hospital until the end, one holding Joe's right hand and the other his left.

The last thing his daughter, Susan, did while there with him was to wipe away a tear running down her father's cheek.

After his midnight death, the two women left the hospital and returned home. Their parish priest soon come to the house, embraced both, helped with phone calls, visited, prayed with the gathering family, and spoke about the funeral liturgy. He left a book which contains the prayers, readings, and prefaces for the Mass of Christian burial as well as explanations of participation by the family in the rite. Their pastor also suggested that they look over the text, and he indicated his openness to any ideas they might have for personal involvement in the funeral service.[1]

Sam's wife, daughter, and other relatives accepted his invitation. Despite the trauma of the event and their fatigue from the ordeal, they spent the next three hours reading and, in particular, praying over the many scriptural passages in that book. The Joseph family found that this process was not merely a mechanical step in planning the burial Mass but, more important, a real help for understanding and coping with their grief.

At the Mass itself, relatives proclaimed the readings, grandchildren brought forward the bread, wine, and several gifts symbolic of Sam's life, while the organist played and sang some Marian music recalling his great love for our Lady.

The second biblical passage, chosen by Sam's daughter for the funeral, reflected those final hospital hours and Susan's last loving gesture for her father: "Then I saw new heavens and a new earth. The former heavens and the former earth had passed away, and the sea was no longer. I also saw a new Jerusalem, the holy city, coming down out of heaven from God, beautiful as a bride prepared to meet her husband. I heard a loud voice from the throne cry out: 'This is God's dwelling among men. He shall dwell with them and they shall be his people and he shall be their God who is always with them. He shall wipe every tear from their eyes, and there shall be no more death or mourning, crying out or pain, for the former world has passed away.'

"The One who sat on the throne said to me, 'See, I make all things new!' " (Revelation 21:1-5).

Mass of Christian Burial

The *Rite of Funerals*, revised according to the directives of the Second Vatican Council, explicitly encourages the presiding priest and parish ministers to do exactly what Sam Joseph's pastor did after the man's death.

The ritual's introduction mentions that in preparing and planning for the celebration "the priest should consider the various circumstances, and in particular the wishes of the family and the community. He should make free use of the choices afforded in the rite."[2]

It goes on in a specific way to remark, "In general, all the texts are interchangeable and may be chosen, with the help of the community or family, to reflect the individual situation."[3]

Finally, it directs the priest to "show loving concern for the family of the deceased person, support them in the time of sorrow, and as much as possible involve them in planning the funeral celebration and the choice of the options made available in the rite."[4]

The Church sees death as a "passage," a journey, or a move from here to eternity. The funeral ritual's introduction expresses that theological view in these words: "In the funeral rites the Church celebrates the paschal mystery of Christ. Those who in baptism have become one with the dead and risen Christ will pass with him from death to life, to be purified in soul and welcomed into the fellowship of the saints in heaven. They look forward in blessed hope to his second coming and the bodily resurrection of the dead.

"The Church therefore celebrates the eucharistic sacrifice of Christ's passover for the dead, and offers prayers and petitions for them. In the communion of all Christ's members, the prayers which bring spiritual help to some may bring to others a consoling hope."[5]

This notion offers hope for believers and comfort for those who mourn. Such hope and comfort, according to Church directives, should be the goal or outcome of the burial Mass and rites. Thus, "Priests and all others should remember that, when they commend the dead to God in the funeral liturgy, it is their duty to strengthen the hope of those present and to foster their faith in the paschal mystery and the resurrection of the dead. In this way the compassionate kindness of Mother Church and the consolation of the faith may lighten the burden of believers without offending those who mourn."[6]

There are various elements of the funeral celebration that dramatize, ritualize, or symbolize reasons which give us hope in the midst of death and comfort during our grief.

• *The color of the priest's vestments.* We normally associate the color white with Easter, weddings, baptisms, events of joy, happiness, and victory. Since we are not merely grieving over a loved one's loss but also celebrating his or her entrance through death into life forever, generally the clergy wear white vestments instead of black or purple.

• *Music.* More than anything else in worship, music affects our feelings and the atmosphere in which we pray. It expresses well our inner thoughts. Rather than the customary funeral melodies which tend to be heavy and sad, the hymns and songs are light and joyful. Easter tunes which speak of the Lord's resurrection are particularly appropriate.

• *Passages from the Bible.* Among the many options open to us in the funeral liturgy is a list of nearly fifty scriptural readings. We may select three: one from the Old Testament, one from the Epistles, and one from the Gospels.

If we have a scriptural text not included in this list which seems particularly appropriate, we are free to select it for the Mass.

• *The Easter, or paschal, candle.* For fifty days, starting on Easter Sunday, the large paschal candle stands in the sanctuary. It symbolizes the risen Christ and tells us he has conquered sin and death and now lives in our midst. In the revised Catholic funeral service we carry this candle in procession or place it before the casket as a reminder that the deceased, through his or her death, shares in that victory of Jesus over the powers of darkness.

• *Sprinkling of the casket.* We first share in the resurrection of the Lord through baptism. At the font, saving waters poured over our body made us a Christian and our whole being a new creation filled with the Holy Spirit. When the priest sprinkles holy water over the casket during the service, this gesture should recall that initial washing in baptism. It is baptism which gives us the basis for hope in the personal rising of loved ones to life forever.

• *Incensing of the body.* As Christians, we believe the body is a temple of the Holy Spirit and one day will be resurrected by God's mighty power. After and/or during Mass, the priest walks around the casket and incenses the body as a sign of our respect for the remains of our loved one and as a final farewell or commendation of the departed individual to God.

• *Presentation of gifts.* The Church encourages us at the funeral Mass to bring to the altar the bread and wine and perhaps some gifts symbolic of a beloved's life. This action in effect says, "Lord, we give our loved one back to you. We accept your will. We know it is some event in your plan. We thank you for the gift of our beloved's entire life." Here are some symbolic gifts which have been used in recent funerals to express the main interests, loves, and efforts of a deceased person: a wedding photo; a family portrait; a familiar rosary, crucifix, and prayerbook; a carpenter's hammer; a saxophone player's sheet music; a nurse's cap; a certificate of appreciation for service given upon retirement. These can be placed on a small table before or near the altar.

• Holy communion. Reception of the Eucharist is the most perfect way to share in the funeral Mass. The Church encourages those present to receive communion and even to do so under both kinds or from the cup. While everyone receives the whole Christ under the form of bread alone, it is a better and fuller sign that we truly do eat and drink the Lord's body and blood when we communicate from the chalice as well. The words of Jesus in

John 6:54 have great meaning here: "He who feeds on my flesh and drinks my blood has life eternal, and I will raise him up on the last day."

• *The ceremony after Mass and at the cemetery is called a liturgy of final farewell and commendation.* In some ways, this is the most difficult time, for it is a final good-bye to one we have loved through life. But again the support of friends and the comfort of faith tell us that although it is a good-bye, it isn't final. A separation, yes — but only a temporary one. An end, yes — but, at the same time, a beginning. The following prayer, one of several suggested to conclude the graveside service, summarizes these thoughts:

God, your days are without end,
    your mercies beyond counting.
Help us always to remember
    that life is short
and the day of our death is known to you alone.
May your Holy Spirit lead us
    to live in holiness and justice all our days.
Then, after serving you in the fellowship of your
        Church,
with strong faith, consoling hope, and perfect love for
    all,
may we joyfully come to your kingdom.
We ask this through Christ our Lord. Amen.[7]

To involve the deceased's family in preparation of the funeral liturgy takes time for the parish priest or pastoral minister, and that time can't be programmed or planned. The essential element is calling upon the survivors almost immediately after the death of their beloved.

This visit, like the midnight appearance of the pastor at Sam Joseph's house, in itself brings great comfort to the bereaved. But, moreover, if offers the family both the impetus and the resources necessary to engage in the preparation for the Mass of Christian burial — an activity which they probably would not undertake on their own.

The very involvement of all, again as in the Joseph family's situation, not only results in a more personal burial service but also exerts a considerable healing impact upon the participants.

A parish in Cincinnati recognizes the value of this involved preparation process. It, however, simultaneously grasps the difficulty involved for the clergy or pastoral ministers of a large parish to make that necessary immediate visit. To achieve this desired goal and to overcome that real obstacle, leaders formed a bereavement committee of about twenty people.

As soon as the group is notified about a parishioner's death, one member quickly calls the nearest survivor's home and offers to stop over. During the subsequent visit, the committee's representative determines what the survivor or survivors may need (food, child care, telephone calls, transportation, liturgy preparation, etc.). He or she then contacts pertinent people of the bereavement group who see to it that these concerns are cared for by competent volunteers.

This is a most pragmatic committee. The members know, for example, that "in many urban areas, the newspaper obituary column serves as a kind of classified advertising for burglars. A person to stay in the house during visitation and funeral services not only insures against unwelcome intrusion, but relieves the bereaved of this anxiety."[8] The bereavement unit will provide just such a "watch person" for that purpose.

The quotation in the previous paragraph is from a book by Carol Luebering, a charter member of that committee, which describes the operation of their bereavement unit and how similar ones could be established in other parishes.

Consolation for the Grieving

Dr. Troy Organ is professor emeritus of philosophy at Ohio University, Athens. In *The Christian Century*, an ecumenical weekly, he describes what happened on a golden autumn day in 1978:[9]

The sun shone in my eyes at the breakfast table, and I asked my wife, Lorena, to pull the curtains on her side of the table. Over breakfast we chatted about the evening before — we had been to a party, and I had not seen her so radiant for months. I noted a few lumps in the cooked cereal — a phenomenon most unusual in the 40 years she had been cooking for me, but a matter too inconsequential to be mentioned on this warm, sunny morning. After breakfast she drove me to the university for my eight o'clock class. As I got out of the car I gave her a pat, saying: "I'll be home for lunch. I want to take a short nap before my afternoon class."

"See you at noon," she replied, and drove off.

By 11 o'clock the day was so warm that I shed my coat as I walked the mile from my office to our home. I noticed that the garage door was down. Perhaps Lorena had closed it to keep the house a bit cooler. When I found the front door locked, I pushed the doorbell. I was prepared to greet her with "Lady, I'm the Fuller brush salesman," or "I'm selling Bibles to work my way through college." But she did not come to open the door for me. I walked around the house and entered through the back door.

"I'm home, dear," I shouted as I opened the door off the patio. The silence puzzled me. In the kitchen I found no preparations for lunch, although the breakfast dishes had been washed. The bed was made, and the rooms were in perfect order. I noted that the door to our attached garage was closed. When I opened it, a blast of hot blue air hit me. The odor of exhaust fumes

137

was overpowering. Then I saw Lorena slumped behind the steering wheel of the car. I rushed to open the garage door and shouted to a neighbor to call an ambulance and the police. Then I discovered that the ignition was on, though the motor had stopped. I began to shake her body, but saw at once that there was no life. I realized that the motor had run until all oxygen had been exhausted. My wife had committed suicide.

Lorena had suffered from recurrent periods of mental depression during the past 12 years, had undergone shock therapy, and had spent six weeks in a mental health center in an effort to learn which anti-depression medication could help her. In two previous bouts with depression, medicine had turned the tide. She had been physically better during the summer. Almost every day she had swum a mile and jogged more than a mile. We had played many rounds of golf. I had hoped that the autumn of social activities would stimulate her to the enjoyment of living. Of course, I knew that she had been having difficulties doing the common tasks like cooking, shopping, sewing and writing letters. Even talking with friends required too much effort. Only a few months earlier she had assured the psychiatrist that she would not try to take her own life, because, as she said, "It is not right." Although I had heard her say to herself many times, "I wish I were dead," she told me when I challenged her that she would never try to end her life.

[Within a few minutes an ambulance arrived, paramedics took her body to the hospital and eventually a neighbor drove Dr. Organ there.]

The doctor came. "We tried to save her, but we couldn't."

"I know," I said. "I want to see her."

"But that is most unusual," I was told. I responded with enough emotion to destroy all resistance.

138

After a few minutes I was allowed to be in the room alone with her. I kissed her forehead, removed her wedding and engagement rings, and took one last look. The neighbor drove me home, insisting that I must eat to keep up my strength, but roast beef and corn on the cob were more than I could handle. I settled for a dish of applesauce. The meal was interrupted by the funeral director, who was taken aback when I told him that I wanted cremation, I did not want the ashes returned, and I did not want a funeral service. I telephoned our two children, and returned to our home.

Friends poured in all afternoon. There were never less than a dozen people with me during the rest of the day. As each arrived, there was a brief expression of sorrow, and then conversation turned to the weather, politics and university gossip. I wanted to talk about Lorena, but everyone else seemed to find this an embarrassing topic. Almost every half-hour someone arose to make another pitcher of iced tea. By early evening my son had arrived, and I had an excuse to remove myself from the assembly of well-wishers.

* * *

The well-meaning neighbors tried to console Dr. Organ in his tragic, unanticipated loss; but they failed to be as effective as they might have been. While working through his grief in the struggle to "return to the joy in living," the Ohio professor gained insights "not only on how to grieve but also on how to give consolation."

His recommendations and the others which follow below should help reassure uneasy visitors to the bereaved and make their calls a source of great comfort to those burdened with grief.

• *Understand some of the attitudes, feelings, or actions often experienced or carried out by grieving people.* There has been an enormous amount of literature published over the past decade about the grieving process. One need not be an expert to stop at a neighbor's home immediately after the death, pay respects at the formal calling hours, or later visit a widow or widower. But it can help to possess an elemental awareness that disbelief, shock, sobbing, denial, confusion, panic, bargaining, depression, guilt, anger, preoccupation, loneliness, despair, sadness, helplessness, frustration, envy, hatred, bitterness or resentment, hope, missing the loved one, and the struggle to adopt new life patterns are natural, common, and expected elements in the journey through grief.[10]

It might help as a simplification of this to remember that there is a parallel between the stages of dying and the patterns of grieving.

• *Know that grief tends to come in waves — huge and frequent at the beginning — engulfing us less often and not so intensely as time moves on.* When a large ship passes by, the immediate waves caused by the vessel may swallow us up; but they subside in a moment or two and we surface until the next comes along. As the boat vanishes from sight, so too the waves ebb — and lesser ones or none at all trouble us.

Experienced ocean swimmers know this. When a wall of water approaches, they dive through or ride with the wave, understanding that they will be temporarily engulfed but will naturally rise to air and light as the wave passes.

Inexperienced swimmers may panic in the process, and fear that they will be forever covered by the water and never see light or breathe air again; in other words, they fear they will drown. In their panic and fear they may aggravate the situation by frantically flailing about or fighting the wave.

Grief is like a wave of water. It normally starts in the stomach and from there we can almost feel its progress as the sad feeling rises to the top and engulfs us, perhaps even leading us to tears. But all feelings are ephemeral, and grief is no exception. In time the heavy sadness subsides, like a wave, and we can breathe again, almost feel normal for a while — until the next wave.

Immediately after a death experience we may not discern the wavelike nature of grief. We are often numb with shock, devastated by the event, and seemingly submerged in or overwhelmed by the sadness of our loss. But within a few hours the pattern of waves may emerge, and to understand that fact can help us enormously to deal with the grief. With that knowledge, we see ourselves as normal, not neurotic; we remain calm during the wave, conscious it will pass, and we find courage to endure the succession of grief waves, aware that their frequency and intensity will most likely diminish in time.

I spent some time on a Sunday afternoon with Mary Jones following the murder of her brilliant lawyer-son the night before. She sat, almost frozen in her chair, stared straight ahead, responded not at all, and seemingly heard nothing as I spoke about the waves of grief to this fine lady with beautiful white hair. A half hour later, however, as the family and I sipped drinks and talked about many other things, Mary suddenly remarked, "I am feeling a wave."

• *Listen with love.* The kind of reflective listening we recommended for visits to the sick and the dying is also powerfully effective for those who are grieving.

Dr. Organ described how many times "in offices and homes, while jogging with friends on streets and roads, and while sharing a meal in a restaurant," he recounted the experiences of that fateful day. Simply by describing to another interested listener what happened — breakfast together, the final words exchanged, coming home, the strange empty house, moving throughout the home, opening the garage door, seeing his wife there, shouting to neighbors for help and all the painful subsequent experiences — seemed to help.

This man, crushed by his wife's suicide, has some advice for us about the value of this listening: "I am normally introspective, but throughout the healing process I poured out my grief to friends and strangers. It was a necessary purgation. . . . I wanted the other person to listen. Grief can be resolved, but not if it is ignored, forgotten or hidden. It must be brought into the open. It must be relived and shared both verbally and emotionally. . . .

"There is consolation in finding someone to talk to. The listener does not have to offer advice or cite similar experiences he or she may have suffered. The one who grieves needs to talk; he or she is frustrated if the listener seeks to avoid discussing the cause of the grief. Some comforters seem to want to talk about everything except death. . . . This is no time to speak of the love of God. That can come later."[11]

Joseph Bayly would second Organ's remarks and reinforce this principle of "Listen with love." He had three sons — Danny, John, and Joe — and lost all of them at early ages: "One at eighteen days, after surgery; another at five years, with leukemia; the third at eighteen years, after a sledding accident complicated by mild hemophilia."[12]

Mr. Bayly cites an incident after one of those tragedies during which he was comforted by a good listener and burdened by a poor one:

I was sitting, torn by grief. Someone came and talked to me of God's dealings, of why it happened, of hope beyond the grave. He talked constantly, he said things I knew were true.

I was unmoved, except to wish he'd go away. He finally did.

Another came and sat beside me. He didn't talk. He didn't ask leading questions. He just sat beside me for an hour and more, listened when I said something, answered briefly, prayed simply, left.

I was moved. I was comforted. I hated to see him go.[13]

• *Touch with care.* Again, the value of communicating our caring presence by touch, discussed and urged in conjunction with visits to the sick and dying, holds true for those who are grieving.

Joseph Bayly gives some advice on this point based upon what helped him after one of his young sons died: "Don't try to 'prove' anything to a survivor. An arm about the shoulder, a firm grip of the hand, a kiss: these are the proofs grief needs, not logical reasoning."[14]

Troy Organ speaks in a similar vein about the comfort that caring touch brought him after Lorena committed suicide: "Suffering the death of a loved one is a lonely experience. How often have I met a friend who shook my hand when I wanted an arm thrown about my shoulders. If one cannot speak the right words to the one who is hurting, one can at least touch him."[15]

Those real-life testimonies to the value of touch have contemporary scientific corroboration. The *Wall Street Journal* carried this brief item which, while directed to the care physicians give patients, has relevance for those who seek to serve bereaved people: "For ages, medicine men have touched patients as part of the healing process. Modern studies prove a reassuring handshake, palpation or massage by a doctor makes patients feel better. But in today's high-tech medicine patients are touched less, complains an essayist in *The New England Journal of Medicine.* Some elderly suffer 'skin starvation,' he says. And in the intensive care ward, 'that Faustian soul of modern technology,' patients are touched only by 'electrodes, wires, tubes, scopes and the like.'

"A world-wide survey of 169 medical schools by a New Zealand psychologist finds only 12 — five in the U.S.

— that teach the value and technique of touching. His school, Otago University, offers fledgling doctors a five-week course in touching. One result: More young doctors and nurses there use massage on newborns, senile and psychiatric patients."[16]

• *Allow the grieving person to weep.* Dr. Organ puts it this way: "Again, weeping has its role in the healing process. It is helpful to weep with another. Even if the other does not weep, it is healing to be able to weep unashamedly in the presence of another. We must cease assuming that weeping is a feminine activity. Men also need to weep."[17]

• *Remember that grief lasts for life.* Troy Organ found that one of the cruelest remarks made to him by well-meaning comforters was: "In time your grief will end."

The waves indeed become less mountainous and less frequent, but they never pass away. Instead they surprise us at irregular and usually unexpected moments.

Something external like a picture, a song, or a holiday can trigger tears and a wave of sadness.

One woman compared this to an onion. Peel off a layer and you cry for awhile until the pungent odor seems to lose its power. Peel off another skin and the process starts all over again.

Grieving people frequently question their own sanity, maturity, or self-discipline when these periodic surges of grief arrive. They judge that by now — a few months after the death — their grief should be gone. Such judgments are inaccurate and too harsh. The reemergence of tears or sadness simply indicates the depth of love present, the extent of the loss, and the fact that another level or layer of painful sadness needs healing.

• *Show active, useful, and specific concern.* Dr. Organ speaks from his own experience of this: "Perhaps the consolation I most resented in the early weeks of my

144

mourning was the well-intended promise: 'Call me any time you need help.' Naturally I never called. Such counselors ought to know that the time to give help is now, not later. Grief is a helplessness that does not cry for help. One cries — and hopes that help will come unbidden. Those who say, 'I'll have you over to dinner sometime,' and then offer no invitation, increase rather than diminish grief. How much I appreciated a friend who said to me: 'You are to be my guest every Thursday evening at 6:30. I have already set aside a napkin ring for you.' "[18]

• *Eventually put closure on the grief process.* Talking about the death event helps ease the pain for grieving people. We have seen how that was the case with Dr. Organ in dealing with his wife's suicide. Consequently, people wishing to assist the bereaved need to practice well the art of active, interested listening.

However, the talking and thinking of those burdened with grief tend to move in circles. Their words and thoughts naturally weave around and around the same issue and never get off the point.

While this type of speaking and pondering has its own healing value, there eventually comes a time when the bereaved must move on, break out of the circle, and go forward with life.

Judith Tate, who helped develop and promote the "Beginning Experience," a weekend effort to deal with grief for the widowed or divorced, has written about that need for closure. In her book *Learning to Live Again* she notes: "They are chained to the past when they spend too much time reliving it in their memories, when they use the past to excuse unsuitable present behavior, when they ignore the present and refuse to face the future.

"In any case, as long as people remain emotionally bound to a person or event of the past, they cannot get on very well with living in the here and now. They keep spinning around the same circle."[19]

At some point in time, closure is required. The grieving individual needs gently but firmly to close the door on the past. Trying to slam it shut with fierce, angry determination will not do. The door simply springs open again. Weakly and indecisively nudging it closed also will not work. The door remains open. The bereaved must make a gentle, definite, firm, and decisive move to put closure on the past.

Tate outlines the three elements of that closure decision: "Closure requires a decision to do three things: first, to accept the past for what it is; second, to shift into a kind of emotional neutral gear concerning the past; and third, to become actively involved in new life in the present."[20]

There is no precise and no predictable time when a person should take this step of closure; nor is there some one obvious person who should help motivate the bereaved to make that move.

The grieving individual may come to such a decision on his or her own. Making the "Beginning Experience" weekend has been, for many, an occasion facilitating the necessary closing of doors. For still others, a strong but loving word from some caring friend may prompt closure.

The title of a song by Neil Diamond nicely expresses this closure decision in a graphic and poetic way: "Come Dry Your Eyes Now."

The parish priest visited Ann George daily during the last few weeks of her life on earth. But throughout the year following her death, he never once stopped at the George home to comfort the bereaved husband. He saw, spoke to, or waved at him on weekends at Mass; but new Anns, new dying people, new deaths — all these claimed his time and prevented what would have been deeply appreciated calls to the George home.

146

Perhaps, in my vision of the future, we will one day have a group of volunteer parishioners who can do just that — visit regularly the home of a bereaved spouse, parent, or child. Then the triad would be complete: no Catholic, Christian, or human would ever die, be buried, or grieve alone.

Coping With Our Losses

Earl Frawner, born in Oklahoma of Indian heritage, became a construction contractor boring holes under highways for telephone cables and water lines, married Nancy, fathered three children, and, at thirty-five, was a divorced man.

He tells the story of the fateful day when the final break came, beginning with his long-distance telephone call home the evening before:

The conversation started as it did every night, with light talk. And then it turned suddenly serious when she said I was overdrawn at the bank and was late on some equipment payments. That news was not totally unexpected, but still I was in no mood to hear any more about it. I knew that in one week the job I was working on would be completed and I would have all the money I needed to catch up. These thoughts were going through my mind as Nancy kept talking, and I almost missed what she said next: "I don't want to live with you any more."

A sudden sick feeling was in my stomach and I felt my shoulders sag as if a good amount of weight was added to them. I was numb and speechless. It was nine o'clock at night and she was three hundred miles away. I told her not to say anything more, that I would be home as soon as possible.

On that drive home, I thought of the things I would tell her. I would tell her that I loved her — something I had not said for eight years.

147

Eight years before, Nancy had divorced me for one day. She had said then that she didn't love me and that the only reason she had ever said she did was because I made her say it. I had been hurt, and I determined never to make her say it again. If I wouldn't tell her I loved her, she wouldn't feel like she had to say she loved me. I did slip once, one night while making love. But that was the only time I said it in eight years.

Driving home I realized how childish I had been. It was a game we had played, and a cruel game it was. I decided that when I got home, I would express my feelings for her in a way I had never done before.

During that drive home I started having a lot of negative feelings about myself. We had gotten back from Alaska only seven months before. The six months we spent there ended in financial disaster. I lost all that I had made in the previous five years.

Going to Alaska had been a childhood dream. It was my dad's dream, and he never made it. So when I had the opportunity to go, I sold my business and left with dreams of making my fortune. I think I could have made it, but Nancy was so unhappy there that I decided to come back. We came home penniless. It had been my decision to go, so I had to blame myself for the outcome.

During the seven months we had been back, I had not shown myself any mercy at work. I was working 90 hours a week, and I didn't intend to let up until I had regained all that we had lost.

I decided that when I got home, I would tell Nancy not only that I loved her very much but also that I would soon make her a rich woman. While I was at it, I would tell her I would stop gambling. I had gambled ever since I was a boy; and the more I won, the more I bet. When I would lose, Nancy would be upset. So I would quit.

With all these proposals in my head, I began to feel a lot better because there just wasn't any way she could turn me down.

I was wrong. When I got home, I felt the misery and heartache so deep down that I knew it would be a long time before I was rid of it.

My wife didn't love me. That was the reason for my divorce. She said that I was a good person, a good father and a good provider, and that it didn't seem right for me to have to go through life with someone who didn't care for me. Her words came out as soft as possible, but they were too hard for me to take.

I tried to convince Nancy that I really didn't require a lot of love and that I had enough for both of us. She lay very still in bed while I told her how I had felt for her since we were both 14 years old. I talked about all the good times we had had in our almost 15 years of marriage. I told her how much our three kids meant to me and how secure I felt at home with my family.

The only reply was silence. I realized my marriage was over, and I cried.

The next day I wanted to eat one last meal together with my family. My belongings were all packed and loaded, and I was supposed to leave right after supper. I knew that I would have to tell my kids goodbye, but I didn't know how I would do it when the time came.

At the supper table everyone was quite solemn. None of us had a lot to say. I would get choked up; my eyes would water; my nose would run; and I couldn't talk. Finally I couldn't take it any longer, and I made my break for the door. I had made up my mind that my kids would not see me cry.

As I made my run for my pickup, my kids were in close pursuit. And by now I was totally out of control. My children had now seen a grown man cry, and that man was their father. My oldest son, Allen, stood on the porch with his head hung down. My little girl, Susan, was on the sidewalk with her face in her hands. And my baby, Jay, was hanging on the door handle of my pickup screaming, "Daddy, don't leave."

By then I couldn't say anything. I broke Jay's grip on the door and drove away. In my mirror, I could see him chasing me and then falling down. I knew that he was also crying because the best buddy he ever had had just left home.[21]

* * *

It is difficult not to weep over the plight of this man, his children, and his wife as well. But how many Earls and Nancys do we have in the world today? I would judge that every reader of these lines has at least one close relative or friend who could relate a similar tale of conflict, hurts, separation, divorce, and loss.

We have mentioned earlier the research of Dr. Elisabeth Kübler-Ross on the stages of dying and their additional parallel application to those who care for the critically ill as well as to those who are grieving.

Subsequent reflection has led many to realize that these same stages, attitudes, feelings, or actions apply also to people suffering any kind of deep personal loss. That, obviously, is the situation of two people whose marriage seems headed for disaster or which has already failed.

However, we can see those elements active in such other diverse contexts as losing a job, finding your house burglarized or burned, moving from one area to another, realizing your life's dream may never materialize, watching your youth disappear, seeing your church renovated, having a beloved parish priest transferred, leaving a community of friends, feeling or believing that the traditions of Catholicism are being swept away, undergoing a mastectomy, knowing your old neighborhood is no more. The list could go on and on

Willy Malarcher works as a liturgical artist. He frequently speaks on behalf of a pastor before the parish council or some other gathering of people about renewing the interior of a church according to the principles of the Second Vatican Council. For some years the hostility and generally adverse reaction of the listeners puzzled him. He then read Dr. Kübler-Ross's *On Death and Dying* and realized his audience was moving through a death/grieving process. Moreover, his listeners viewed him as the terrible death-dealing agent.

This "wicked" man from outside was, in their judgment, threatening to injure, destroy, and take away elements dear to them for many years. The railing where the parishioners knelt, the statues they admired, the font in which they were baptized — all these and other things were in danger of being modified or removed. The prospect of such tampering by this man caused them to lash out at him and others connected to him with anger, denial, bargaining, and sadness.

Simply being aware of this helped Malarcher deal with the opposition and even rejection he so frequently experienced; it also aided him in planning a strategic approach which could aid the parishioners to recognize and to cope with their own sense or feelings of personal loss.

Paula Ripple spent some half dozen years as executive director of the North American Conference of Separated and Divorced Catholics. During the course of this labor she wrote *The Pain and the Possibility* as an "affirming and healing guide for the divorced and separated, their parents and relatives, neighbors and friends."[22] Like Judith Tate with the "Beginning Experience" and her book *Learning to Live Again*, Ripple applies the stages of dying to the divorce experience.

To illustrate: One of the coping mechanisms in this process of death, grief, loss, or divorce is denial. We deny the possibility or existence of the death or loss until we can marshal sufficient psychological and spiritual strength to cope with the reality of this trauma. Ripple cites a few cases of such denial before and after the marital breakup:

Roberta told me that the day she received a call from the public health office asking her to come in for a VD check she told the caller that he had the wrong number and hung up. It was only when he called back to check on her name and phone number that she remembered that every day for the past several weeks, when she opened the cabinet in the bathroom, she had looked at a bottle of an antibiotic that she knew her husband was taking. She was a nurse and knew what the antibiotic was for. She denied it even to herself.

Marie struggled with her own disbelief at the extent of her denial mechanism. She had picked up her husband's wallet one day and had found there a contraceptive. She then promptly put the incident out of her mind ... knowing full well that they never used them. . . . What frightened her most was the extent of her total surprise when her husband finally told her that he was leaving and that there was someone else in his life. So completely had she blocked what she did not want to know. . . . So complete was her denial.

Bill told me that he had gone to a travel agent to make reservations for a trip to the Caribbean for him and his wife to celebrate their 25th wedding anniversary even though she had already moved out and had the papers served for the divorce.

One couple I know has been separated for more than six months. They still go home to his parents and to hers for holidays and other family celebrations. They have told no one that they are separated.[23]

Paula Ripple sees the possibility of healing and growth or deterioration and death in going through the denial and other stages of the grief process. With Judith

Tate, she knows that ultimately people who suffer personal loss must put some degree of closure upon the past and begin to live the present. There will always be bittersweet memories, and the grief or pain never totally vanishes. But the death and resurrection Jesus taught and lived holds true for more than our final death at the end of this earthly life. We experience countless little and large deaths throughout our time here: major traumas like a divorce and minor losses like leaving home for college.

But God wishes us also to taste countless little and large resurrections. Unless we die, we cannot rise. However, if we can live with and then finally let go of the deep personal loss, a new and fuller life awaits us.

12

The Ultimate Healing, Or Why Bad Things Happen to Good People

After spending many years in New England as a Catholic school religion teacher, a classmate of mine became pastor of a fairly large parish.

Unfortunately, this brilliant man, now in his early fifties, worked too hard for — and worried too much about — his flock.

The excessive work and worry brought on an ulcer which he ignored. That neglect only allowed the stomach disorder to worsen. Finally, one day, weakened by loss of blood he collapsed; an ambulance was called and he was carried out of the rectory on a stretcher.

At one point in the subsequent surgery and recuperative period, my classmate slipped into an extended coma and had, in his judgment, a death-and-return-to-life experience. His comments about the bright, warm light he saw at the end of a tunnel and the great serenity he felt during those moments parallel the testimonies of others who similarly have suffered bodily death and recovered.

This classmate and friend, semiretired and living in Florida, remarked to me at lunch one day that as a result of his unique experience he no longer has any fears about dying. The God he will face after death seems, in his view, to be a personal being of light, warmth, and love before whom no one should be frightened. In some ways, we could characterize that kind of God as a loving parent waiting with open arms for the return of a son or daughter.

* * *

Dr. Raymond A. Moody studied about one hundred fifty cases of people like my classmate who apparently died, experienced a brief existence after death, and then came back to life as we know it. His subjects came under three categories: persons who were resuscitated after having been thought, adjudged, or pronounced clinically dead by their doctors; persons who, in the course of accidents or severe injury or illness, came very close to physical death; persons who, as they died, told of such an experience to other people present who in turn reported them to Moody.[1]

My classmate's observations paralleled the remarks which those people communicated to Dr. Moody and which served as the basis for his book *Life After Life*.

What they saw or experienced was: a very bright light of unearthly brilliance which did not hurt their eyes in any way, dazzle them, or keep them from seeing other things around them; a personal being of love, warmth, and magnetic attractiveness beyond words; a being who communicated in a remarkable way, made them feel total love and acceptance, rapidly reviewed their entire lives, gently pointed out selfishness and showed how these actions were or could have been occasions for growth in learning to love other people and acquire knowledge.[2]

My priest-friend found his fears about death disappeared for him after this death-life experience. Dr. Moody's respondents not only lost that dread of dying but also had no desire to return to this life, so marvelous was the new mode of existence.

One person spoke about the wonderful nature of that encounter: "It was wonderful over there on the other side, and I kind of wanted to stay. But knowing that I had something good to do on earth, was just as wonderful in a way. So, I was thinking, 'Yes, I must go back and live,' and I got back into my physical body. I almost feel as though I stopped the bleeding myself. At any rate, I began to recover after that."[3]

An older woman found it was so beautiful in the beyond that she no longer wanted to stay here and asked her family to stop their prayers for her continued life on earth. The lady's niece described the situation: "I was with my elderly aunt during her last illness, which was very drawn out. I helped take care of her, and all that time everyone in the family was praying for her to regain her health. She stopped breathing several times, but they brought her back. Finally, one day she looked at me and she said, 'Joan, I have been over there, over to the beyond and it is beautiful over there. I want to stay, but I can't as long as you keep praying for me to stay with you. Your prayers are holding me over here. Please don't pray anymore.' We did all stop, and shortly after that she died."[4]

Another individual simply observed, "After I came back, I cried off and on for about a week because I had to live in this world after seeing that one [on the other side]. I didn't want to come back."[5]

Are these accurate descriptions of the reality beyond our human existence on earth? Or are they wishful projections which spring from our imaginations and inner longings? Who can say? How are we to know?

The accounts, amazingly enough, *do* correspond to the traditional Catholic theological speculation about life after death in the joys of heaven. They also mirror the writings of several contemporary religious writers on this topic.[6]

Such prospects of a beautiful existence beyond the pain, loneliness, rejections, tragedies, disasters, and hurts of this earthly life certainly do offer comfort and hope for those crushed by such burdens.

In Chapter 5 we saw that Rabbi Harold Kushner — in trying to fit together his understanding of a good God with the bad thing that happened to his son, Aaron — acknowledges the possibility that such a heaven of beauty beyond could sustain some people suffering through their doubts over a personal disaster. He also believes personally that "the part of us which is not physical, the part we call the soul or personality does not and cannot die." Moreover, his daughter dreamed, following his teenage son's death, that "she had died and was welcomed into heaven by her brother, now grown normal, and by her grandmother (who had died the year before)."

Nevertheless, Kushner maintains that "we have no way of knowing whether these visions are intimations of reality or products of our own wishful thinking." Furthermore, while belief in a world to come can help suffering people endure without losing faith, the rabbi judges that it also can be an excuse for others not to do something about injustice or troubles in this life. He consequently concludes and states his own philosophy about bad things and good people: "The dictate of practical wisdom for people in our situation might be to remain mindful of the possibility that our lives continue in some form after death, perhaps in a form our earthly imaginations cannot conceive of. But at the same time, since we cannot know for sure, we would be well advised to take this world as seriously as we can, in case it turns out to be the only one we will ever have, and to look for meaning and justice here."[7]

It is this point that Rabbi Kushner causes theological difficulty for some. As we noted earlier in the book, he helps us understand that humans, not God, cause many obvious sufferings in our world. To blame God for the terrible deaths or maimings due to a terrorist bombing or for the painful demise brought on by years of excessive drinking is to forget that our Creator endows us with marvelous freedom and allows us to use or abuse such liberty. The alternative, of course, is to take away the very humanness that makes it possible for us to seek, choose, and love one another and the Lord.

The truly thorny issues, however, revolve around tragedies — for example, loss of life as a result of earthquakes or hurricanes — which appear not to stem from human choice. Rabbi Kushner, again as noted before, attributes these and other similar calamities to "bad luck," "fate," or some "inflexible natural laws," all of which are divorced from God. In his desire to preserve the goodness of the Creator amid the badness of life, he seeks "for meaning and justice here."

It is this here-and-now, divorced-from-God approach which has brought forth considerable criticism.

A Boston College professor of psychology, reviewing Kushner's book in the weekly Catholic journal *America*, addresses one of the objections — the rabbi's time-bound attempt to deal with these issues: "The underlying problem with Kushner's analysis is that, despite his backhanded defense of God, he writes from within a time-bound framework. This life is all we know. The good for man begins and ends with this world. Anything else is 'wishful thinking.' If that is so, then it seems to me that others (such as Schopenhauer) have looked at suffering in a more courageous and unblinking fashion. 'The dead,' writes Kushner, 'depend on us for their redemption and immortality.' Yet by 'immortality,' he clearly means living on in memory. And how long do any but the famous live on in memory? And what will become of their memory when the whole race is gone as someday it must? A really honest view compels us to admit that, if there is no ultimate meaning, there is no meaning at all. If this life is the whole show, it will not matter in the long run whether you die accidentally at 18 or peacefully at 80.''[8]

If Rabbi Kushner's analysis — which limits our answers about life's tragedies to this life and effectively removes God from them — leaves something to be desired, how do we make sense out of those difficulties and cope with them? What does our biblical heritage and long Catholic tradition have to teach us about various kinds of sickness and suffering?

Here are some guidelines helpful to me and in my judgment reflective of Catholic theological principles:

• *We bring on much suffering by our own sinfulness and mistaken decisions.* God has endowed us with freedom and allows us, for the sake of that liberty, to follow poor courses of action and make bad choices which ultimately cause trouble and pain for ourselves and for others.

• *Others cause us suffering by their actions which may or may not be sinful.* These commissions or omissions may be deliberate and sinful or unintended and not malicious, but they still hurt us in some way.

In both these instances, God allows but does not directly will and wish the harmful actions.

• *God wishes to eliminate through us human pain and suffering.* Rabbi Kushner is right: hope for answers and relief in heaven should not blind us to injustices on earth nor keep us from doing all we can to eliminate suffering in our midst. In earlier chapters we have cited both biblical texts and the Church's official teaching in support of this approach. Jesus healed and continues to heal today; but he normally does this through material human processes and the efforts of competent, dedicated health-care personnel.

• *Much suffering, once attributed to inexplicable forces beyond us, is discovered later to*

159

have a human origin. I watched my mother suffer through two most difficult ordeals with cancer. Little was known then about what caused cancer and little, if anything, seemed truly to cure the disease. My understanding today is that some research people judge cancer as an illness of our specific age brought on by contemporary diets and lifestyles. The kind of foods we eat, the pace of life we follow, and the stress of our existence, for example, may provoke the illness. If that speculation is correct, my mother's death was not the result of something beyond us but rather the effect of our own choices about how we decide to live in this world. I am not implying that my mother ate or lived sinfully, but merely that as a part of the twentieth century she followed a way of living and dwelt in an environment developed in complex fashion by the human choices of millions. Such a style of life and milieu may have caused or aggravated her cancer. Again, God allows all of this without directly willing the negative consequences.

• *Those tragedy-producing events, like earthquakes, tornadoes, and hurricanes, apparently divorced from human control, are mysteries which we cannot fathom but still fit somehow into God's overall plan of love for us.* God is beyond us, infinite and essentially incomprehensible; so too God's creation, insofar as it shares in that divine character, can never be fully understood. As limited creatures, we do have to stand back in awe and uncertainty at times.

• *God's goodness, love, and concern for us is absolutely certain, unconditional, and all-embracing.* The teaching of Scripture, the example of Jesus, and the experiences of humans over the centuries give repeated and ample testimonies about this. The mysterious and inexplicable nature of the tragedies caused by, for example, a typhoon, needs to be always seen in the light of and balanced off by this sure awareness of God's love.

• *The Lord is actively present in our midst working on and with and through us for our good and the good of others.* It would seem Rabbi Kushner and the others discussed in Chapter 5 have some difficulty with such a concept. However, our constant Catholic tradition — as presented briefly in this book — believes in God's intervention with humankind, holds that prayer (even if in a mysterious manner) can achieve spiritual and physical healing, and provides liturgical rituals echoing that belief for the sick, the dying, and those in any way hurting.

• *God brings good out of everything in our lives, even — perhaps especially — our sins, mistakes, and troubles.* Enrico Garzilli wrote a song in 1970, based on the New Testament (specifically, Romans 8), which starts out: "For to those who love God, who are called in his plan, everything works out for good, and God himself chose them to bear the likeness of his Son that he might be the first of many, many brothers." While the lack of inclusive language poses some problems for that hymn today, it effectively captures the notion of this principle. In my former parish we found that the song offered strong musical support for the bereaved at a funeral.[9]

With a bit of reflection we can cite countless human illustrations of this principle. Natural disasters elicit great outpourings of generosity from concerned people. Rejection leads a disappointed person to another avenue which ultimately proves far better for the once-downcast individual. Repentance after sin finds us more humble before God and compassionate toward others. Disastrous loss of material possessions or good health brings us back to the Lord with a new perspective on this life and the one to come. We must wait for the life beyond to learn just how constantly and extensively this principle has been in operation.

• *All of life and, in particular, life's troubles are best understood and most successfully endured in the context of the life to come.* It is fundamental for the Christian to recall that we are pilgrims, persons on a journey, temporary residents, people looking for an enduring home beyond. There is great beauty and joy in this earthly life. Moreover, we should strive to make it ever more beautiful and joyous for all. But we do not have a perfect or permanent place on earth. Our longing and seeking must be for something ahead of us.

In Eucharistic Prayer III, which expresses our faith in a worship setting, the presiding priest prays on our behalf for that life to come: "There we hope to share in your glory when every tear will be wiped away. On that day we shall see you, our God, as you are. We shall become like you and praise you forever through Christ our Lord from whom all good things come."

It is there that questions will be completely answered and hurts totally healed.

• *Suffering, borne bravely and with acceptance, possesses a mysterious power to help others.* We have seen how Jesus detested sin and suffering and sought to eliminate both. At the same time he willingly accepted that suffering inflicted upon him by evil people: "My Father, if it is possible, let this cup pass me by. Still, let it be as you would have it, not as I" (Matthew 26:39). Moreover, it was his passion, death, and resurrection which set us free.

Christ tells us we must walk a similar path by taking up our cross daily. St. Paul also remarks, "Even now I find my joy in the suffering I endure for you. In my own flesh I fill up what is lacking in the sufferings of Christ for the sake of his body, the church" (Colossians 1:24).

We need to fight against and try to overcome our own sufferings and those of others. But having done that and facing troubles beyond our control, we can gain courage and hope knowing that these sufferings somehow will bring blessings to others and build up the Church.

• *God always works a healing through prayer but not necessarily a physical one.* It would appear, as we have mentioned, that the Lord for various reasons is working more observable and measurable physical cures in these days than in the recent past. Nevertheless, not every prayer for a healing produces the desired result. Why some are cured and others not is another of those complex mysteries and unresolved inquiries. Why, for example, was Jane's breast cancer apparently healed and Ann George's malignancy not? Why did Rabbi Kushner's son die early and my classmate evidently come back to life?

But even if there is no physical, emotional, or intellectual cure, there will always be an inner spiritual healing.

When grandparents — after Sunday Mass — asked for prayers on behalf of their ailing, newborn twin grandchildren, the priest immediately did so, placing a hand on each grandparent's shoulder. His words and gesture brought tears to their eyes. Nevertheless, one of the infants still died. While their immediate request did not materialize, I am sure that brief intercession brought a new perspective, quieting grace, and strengthening courage to the grandparents.

Father MacNutt, in his book *Healing*, lists eleven reasons why people are not cured.[10] He also points out in another volume that "whenever we speak of healing, I think we must also think (and maybe speak) of death, because death is the ultimate healing."[11]

Sheldon Vanauken and his wife, "Davy," grasped with great understanding all these things from their personal experience. They married, and their radiant love stayed with them for eighteen years as they crossed oceans, settled in England, searched for faith, and eventually found religious fulfillment in Christianity.

But sickness came upon Davy, and a doctor's examination revealed the cause of her illness.

Sheldon brought roses, yellow ones, to the hospital for his beloved on the day their physician announced the diagnosis.

When the nurse had brought a vase and gone again, I sat beside her bed and took her hand. Then I said, "Davy..." She looked at me, and I smiled at her. She smiled back. "Dearling," I said. "This — this illness — is maybe going to mean our parting — for a while." Her hand tightened its grip, but she still smiled. "The doctors say that it means that. But a hundred people are praying for you. C.S. Lewis and Maurice. Peter and Bee, Lew and Mary Ann, Thad, Julian. You are in God's hand, dearling." Despite my will, my eyes filled with tears, but I smiled at her.

She too smiled through tears, and said in a husky voice: "Let all be —" Her voice wavered and she gave a little sob. "— According to His perfect will," she said in a stronger voice. "Yesterday, when you were here, I thought — I thought it might be, well, something bad. Your eyes were unhappy..."

I stood up and leaned over her and put my arms around her. "I love you," I said, "whatever it is to be, for ever." I kissed her wet cheeks, and we just held each other for a little. There were tears on my cheeks, too.

Her condition slowly deteriorated and over many months there were daily yellow roses, regular hospital visits, and countless intimate conversations between Sheldon and Davy.

On a bitter winter night the hospital called Sheldon at home and said that he should come quickly because Davy seemed to be slipping away. He raced through deserted streets to his wife's side. "After we had greeted each other and I had kissed her, she said she was thirsty, and I reached past the yellow roses for the carafe and glass. And I gave her a cup of water in the night — our old symbol of courtesy. Then I prayed one of the prayers we always prayed."

Then Davy prayed. She prayed aloud for the hospital and the doctors by name and the nurses, including [Nurse] St. Joan, asking God's blessing on them all, in Jesus' name. I stroked her hand, looking at her face. I said another prayer; and at the end of it I said: "Davy — I love you for ever." She whispered: "Oh, my dearest!"

There was a long silence, I still stroking her hand. Then she said in a stronger voice: "Oh, God, take me." I knew then with certainty that she understood that she was dying. I said: "Go under the Love, dearling. Go under the Mercy." She murmured: "Amen." And then she said: "Thank you, blessed dearling." I kissed her very lightly, so as not to interfere with her breathing.

Then we were silent. Her lips were slightly parted and her eyes were half-open. Every now and then I dipped a swab into the water and moistened her lips. There was no response. I knew with tearless clarity that she was going. I continued to hold her hand.

[Nurse] St. Joan came quietly in and gave me Davy's wedding ring, taken off when her fingers became so thin. I took [Nurse] St. Joan's hand for a minute, and then she went quietly out. I looked at the ring with its ten tiny diamonds — the ten months we had known each other before we were secretly wed in the thunderstorm. Then I put it on Davy's third finger, saying in a low voice: "With this ring I thee wed . . . for all eternity." I do not know whether she heard; but I think she did, for her fingers tightened the least bit.

Time passed, a long time; and there was no change. Each time she breathed there was a faint moan.

The sky was beginning to lighten a bit in the east. I thought she might be unconscious.

Suddenly her fingers tightened on mine. She said in a clear [but] weak voice: "Oh, dearling, look. . ." She didn't go on, if there was more. I knew that if I said, "What is it?" she would make an effort and go on; but I did not do so. I don't know why I didn't. She might have been saying "look" as one who suddenly understands something, or as one who beholds — what? Her voice was so frail, I could not tell which it was. I wished very much to know; I could have asked her; I did not. And I shall not know this side of eternity, for they were her last words: "Oh, dearling, look. . ."

More time passed. The sky was becoming bright. I was now nearly certain that she was unconscious. I still held her hand, her left hand with the ring on it. I did not wish to hold her to life; I merely wished to be with her. Every now and then I said in a low voice: "I am here, Davy; I am with you." But there was no response.

Then she stirred. There was no change at all in her half-parted lips or eyes or the hand I held. But then her other hand and arm came slowly up from her side. I could not think what she was doing. The hand moved slowly across her. It found my face. She touched my brow and hair, then each eye in turn. Then my mouth. Her fingers moved to each corner of my mouth, as we had always done. And I gave her fingers little corner-of-the-mouth kisses, as we had always done. Then her arm fell slowly back. Past seeing and past speaking, with the last of her failing strength, she had said good-bye.[12]

What did Davy see? Was it that warm, personal being of warmth and love which my classmate experienced during his coma? Was it the beginning glimpse of the risen, glorified Jesus? Was it the preliminary taste of heaven's joys where her pain would be over, her tears dried, her questions answered, and her sorrows ended?

Was it the vision of a beautiful home forever, a permanent dwelling place, where she would be rejoining all her deceased loved ones? Was it the awareness that he whose face she touched in a final good-bye would one day, soon enough, be with her once more?

Paul tells us: "Eye has not seen, ear has not heard, nor has it so much as dawned on man what God has prepared for those who love him" (1 Corinthians 2:9).

In John 14:1-3, Jesus gave to his closest friends and us these words of comfort and hope:

Do not let your hearts be troubled.
Have faith in God
and faith in me.
In my Father's house there are many dwelling places;
otherwise, how could I have told you
that I was going to prepare a place for you?
I am indeed going to prepare a place for you,
and then I shall come back to take you with me,
that where I am you also may be.

As a young priest I recall driving past a storefront church with this large neon sign outside it: "Jesus Heals." The words are true. When we pray with faith, and occasionally without our hardly even asking or believing, Christ heals us: sometimes physically, always spiritually, and — in the end — perfectly. God does indeed mend wounded hearts and bodies.

Notes

Chapter 1

1. Boniface Hanley, O.F.M., *Brother André* (Montreal, Que.: St. Joseph's Oratory, 1979), pp. 16-17, 23-25, 62. This small booklet gives an easy-to-read summary both of Brother André and St. Joseph's Oratory at Mount Royal in Montreal.
2. Henri-Paul Bergeron, C.S.C., *Brother André: The Wonder Man of Mount Royal,* tr. Paul Boudreau, C.S.C. (Montreal, Que.: St. Joseph's Oratory, 1938), p. 102.
3. *Ibid.,* pp. 67-68.
4. Hanley, *op. cit.,* p. 46.
5. Richard P. McBrien, *Catholicism*, study ed. (Minneapolis: Winston Press, 1981), pp. 1155-1156.
6. *Vatican Council II: The Conciliar and Post Conciliar Documents,* ed. Austin Flannery, O.P. (Northport, N.Y.: Costello Publishing Co., 1979), "Dogmatic Constitution on the Church," ch. VII, pp. 407-413.
7. St. Thomas Aquinas, *Summa Theologica* (Westminster, Md.: Christian Classics, 1947), vol. V, p. 2849.

Chapter 2

1. Judy Boros, "Endicott Woman Credits Priest for Curing Her Cancer," Binghampton, N.Y.: *The Saturday Press* (April 7, 1984).
2. From a promotional leaflet, "The Healing and Restoration Ministry," published by Edward J. McDonough, C.SS.R., P.O. Box 299, Boston, MA 02132.
3. *The Saturday Press, op. cit.*
4. *Ibid.*

5. Father Ralph A. DiOrio with Donald Gropman, *The Man Beneath the Gift: The Story of My Life* (New York: William Morrow and Co., Inc., 1980). The description of Father DiOrio herein is basically taken from this book, particularly pp. 13, 18, 143, 149-168.

6. Myles Maynard, "In the Name of Jesus, Run," Ann Arbor, Mich.: *New Covenant* (July/August 1984), pp. 10-11.

Chapter 3

1. Morton T. Kelsey, *Healing and Christianity* (New York: Harper and Row, 1976), pp. 53-55. I am indebted to this fine volume for much of what appears in this section, especially for the author's ch. 4, "The Unique Healing Ministry of Jesus of Nazareth," and ch. 5, "What, How, and Why Did Jesus Heal?"

2. Kelsey, *op. cit.,* pp. 55-57. Kelsey cites this arrangement as the foundation for Ethel Banks's booklet, *The Great Physician Calling.*

3. Donald P. McNeil, Douglas A. Morrison, and Henri J.M. Nouwen, *Compassion* (Garden City, N.Y.: Doubleday and Co., Inc., 1982), pp. 16-17. For a few other illustrations, see Matthew 9:36, Matthew 14:14, Mark 8:2, Matthew 9:27.

4. Kelsey, *op. cit.,* p. 95.

Chapter 4

1. Manuscripts and thus translations vary on the number of these disciples, some listing seventy and others seventy-two. In Numbers 11:16-25, Moses gathered seventy men who would receive a portion of his spirit and thus relieve the overburdened leader. Two additional men, who remained behind at camp, also received a spirit of prophecy (Numbers 11:26-30), thus raising the number to seventy-two. That may explain the seeming discrepancy. See Eugene LaVerdiere, S.S.S., *Luke* (Wilmington, Del.: Michael Glazier, Inc., 1980), pp. 144-148.

2. Francis MacNutt, *The Prayer That Heals: Prayer for*

Healing in the Family (Notre Dame, Ind.: Ave Maria Press, 1981), pp. 45-47.

3. Barbara Leahy Shlemon, Dennis Linn, and Matthew Linn, *To Heal as Jesus Healed* (Notre Dame, Ind.: Ave Maria Press, 1978), pp. 13-15.

Chapter 5

1. Harold S. Kushner, *When Bad Things Happen to Good People* (New York: Avon Books, 1983), pp. 1-5.
2. Kelsey, *op. cit.* [see ch. 3, note 1, above], p. xi.
3. *Ibid.*, p. 9.
4. *Ibid.*, ch. 2, "The Case Against Christian Healing," pp. 8-32.
5. Kushner, *op. cit.*, p. 3.
6. *Ibid.*, p. 4.
7. Kelsey, *op. cit.* [see ch. 3, note 1, above], p. 22.
8. *Ibid.*, p. 23.
9. Charlotte Hays, "The Gift of Healing," Los Angeles: *National Catholic Register* (March 4, 1984), pp. 1, 10.
10. Kelsey, *op. cit.* [see ch. 3, note 1, above], p. 28.
11. *Ibid.*, pp. 29-30.
12. Kushner, *op. cit.*, p. 134.
13. *Ibid.*, p. 129.
14. Eileen Flynn, "How Much Should I Put in the Basket?" Huntington, Ind.: *The Priest* (September 1983), pp. 30-33.

Chapter 6

1. James L. Empereur, S.J., *Prophetic Anointing* (Wilmington, Del.: Michael Glazier, Inc., 1982), pp. 15-18. Charles W. Gusmer, *And You Visited Me: Sacramental Ministry for the Sick and the Dying* (New York: Pueblo Publishing Co., 1984), pp. 5-7. These two excellent contemporary studies of this sacrament have good sections on the history of anointing and are foundations for this chapter.
2. *Study Text 2: Pastoral Care of the Sick and Dying*, rev. ed., 1984, published by the Secretariat, Bishops' Com-

mittee on the Liturgy, National Conference of Catholic Bishops (Washington, D.C.: Office of Publishing Services, U.S. Catholic Conference, 1984), p. 3.

3. Gusmer, *op. cit.*, pp. 7-11.
4. *Study Text 2, op. cit.*, pp. 9-10.
5. Gusmer, *op. cit.*, pp. 21-32.
6. *Ibid.*, pp. 33-37.
7. *Vatican Council II, op. cit.* [see ch. 1, note 6, above], "Constitution on the Sacred Liturgy" ch. III, pars. 73-75, p. 22.

Chapter 7

1. *Pastoral Care of the Sick: Rites of Anointing and Viaticum*, International Committee on English in the Liturgy (Collegeville, Minn.: The Liturgical Press, 1983).
2. *Ibid.*, art. 3, p. 10.
3. *Ibid.*, art. 42, p. 24.
4. *Ibid.*, art. 5, p. 12.
5. *Ibid.*, art. 6, p. 12.
6. *Ibid.*, art. 124, p. 94.
7. *Ibid.*, art. 125, pp. 95-96.
8. *Ibid.*, art. 130, p. 101.
9. *Ibid.*, art. 125, p. 95.
10. *Ibid.*, art. 16, p. 14; art. 99, p. 75.
11. *Ibid.*, art. 8, p. 13.
12. *Ibid.*, arts. 9-15, pp. 13-14; art. 102, p. 76; art. 53, p. 27.
13. *Ibid.*, p. 8; art. 124, p. 94.
14. *Ibid.*, art. 7, p. 12.
15. *Ibid.*, art. 117, p. 84.
16. *Ibid.*, art. 121, p. 91.
17. *Ibid.*, art. 125, p. 96.
18. *Ibid.*, art. 122, p. 91.
19. *Ibid.*, art. 121, p. 91.
20. *Ibid.*, art. 106, p. 77.
21. *Ibid.*, art. 107, p. 77.

22. *Ibid.*, art. 123, p. 93.
23. *Ibid.*, art. 107, p. 78.

Chapter 8

1. *Pastoral Care of the Sick, op. cit.* [see ch. 7, note 1, above], art. 72, p. 50.
2. *Ibid.*
3. *Ibid.*, art. 73, p. 51.
4. *Ibid.*, art. 74, p. 51.
5. *Ibid.*, art. 83, p. 57.
6. *Ibid.*, art. 91, pp. 63-64.
7. *Ibid.*, art. 90, p. 63.
8. *Ibid.*, art. 88, p. 61.
9. *Ibid.*, arts. 73-74, pp. 50-51.
10. *Ibid.*, art. 4, p. 11; art. 32, p. 19.
11. *Ibid.*, art. 43, p. 24.
12. *Ibid.*
13. *Ibid.*, art. 55, p. 30.
14. *Ibid.*, art. 56, p. 30.
15. *Ibid.*, art. 43, p. 24.
16. *Ibid.*, art. 3, p. 11.
17. *Ibid.*, art. 40C, p. 22.
18. *Ibid.*, art. 67, p. 44.
19. *Ibid.*, art. 69A, p. 45.
20. *Ibid.*, art. 70A, p. 46.

Chapter 9

1. Shlemon, Linn, and Linn, *op. cit.* [see ch. 4, note 3, above], pp. 36-37.
2. Francis MacNutt, *Healing* (Notre Dame, Ind.: Ave Maria Press, 1974), p. 167.
3. Joseph M. Champlin, *Together in Peace: Priest's Edition* (Notre Dame, Ind.: Ave Maria Press, 1975), p. 70. This is the formula of absolution taken from the *Rite of Penance* in the approved English translation.

4. Joseph M. Champlin, *Why Go to Confession?* (Los Angeles: Franciscan Communications, 1982), p. 30.
5. *Ibid.*, p. 5.
6. Champlin, *Together in Peace, op cit.*, pp. 167-168. This is from art. 4 of the Introduction to the *Rite of Penance*.
7. *Ibid.*, p. 171, art. 7.
8. David Hilfiker, M.D., "Making Medical Mistakes," New York: *Harper's* (May 1984), pp. 59-65.
9. Champlin, *Why Go to Confession?, op. cit.*, pp. 6-7.
10. Robert Faricy, S.J., *Praying for Inner Healing* (New York: Paulist Press, 1979), p. 7.
11. *Ibid.*, p. 8.
12. *Ibid.*, pp. 8-9.
13. Michael Scanlan, *Inner Healing* (New York: Paulist Press, 1974), pp. 12-13.
14. Fulton J. Sheen, *Treasure in Clay* (Garden City, N.Y.: Doubleday and Co., Inc., 1980), pp. 74-75.
15. Robert H. Schuller, *Self-Esteem* (Waco, Tex.: Word Books, 1982), pp. 14-15, 41.
16. Jim McManus, C.SS.R., *The Healing Power of the Sacraments* (Notre Dame, Ind.: Ave Maria Press, 1984), p. 42.
17. *Ibid.*, p. 118.
18. *Ibid.*, pp. 119-120.
19. *Ibid.*, p. 121.
20. Faricy, *op. cit.*, pp. 10-11.
21. *Ibid.*, p. 11.
22. *Ibid.*, p. 12.
23. *Ibid.*
24. Francis MacNutt, *The Power to Heal* (Notre Dame, Ind.: Ave Maria Press, 1977), pp. 247-249.
25. *Vatican Council II, op. cit.* [see ch. 1, note 6, above], "Constitution on the Sacred Liturgy," ch. I, par. 10, p. 6.
26. MacNutt, *Healing, op. cit.*, pp. 208-231.
27. Dennis Linn and Matthew Linn, *Healing of Memories* (New York: Paulist Press, 1974), p. 11.

Chapter 10

1. *Pastoral Care of the Sick, op. cit.* [see ch. 7, note 1, above], art. 209A, p. 158.
2. *Ibid.,* art. 175, p. 136.
3. *Ibid.,* art. 161, p. 130.
4. *Ibid.,* art. 163, p. 131.
5. *Ibid.,* art. 166, pp. 131-132.
6. *Ibid.,* art. 177, p. 136.
7. *Ibid.,* art. 179, p. 137.
8. *Ibid.,* art. 180, p. 137.
9. *Ibid.,* art. 181, pp. 137-138.
10. *Ibid.,* art. 183, p. 138.
11. *Ibid.,* art. 207, p. 156.
12. *Ibid.,* art. 215, p. 162.
13. *Ibid.,* art. 212, p. 162.
14. *Ibid.,* art. 215, p. 163.
15. Elisabeth Kübler-Ross, *On Death and Dying* (New York: Macmillan, 1969).
16. Joseph M. Champlin, *Together by Your Side* (Notre Dame, Ind.: Ave Maria Press, 1979). An audio-cassette kit from the same publisher and by the same name with the subtitle "A Program on How to Comfort the Sick, the Dying and the Bereaved" describes in detail with many examples and suggestions how the ministry to the sick can be carried out. It also provides a training suggestion for forming the kind of volunteers to serve the dying, bereaved, and grieving recommended in later parts of this book.
17. *Pastoral Care of the Sick, op. cit.* [see ch. 7, note 1, above], arts. 216, 221, 222.
18. *Ibid.,* art. 221D, p. 185.
19. *Ibid.,* art. 222, p. 188.

Chapter 11

1. Joseph M. Champlin, *Through Death to Life: Preparing to Celebrate the Mass of Christian Burial* (Notre Dame, Ind.: Ave Maria Press, 1979).

2. *The Rites* (New York: Pueblo Publishing Co., 1976), art. 23, p. 659.

3. *Ibid.,* art. 23:1, p. 659.

4. *Ibid.,* art. 25:3, p. 660.

5. *Ibid.,* art. 1, p. 652.

6. *Ibid.,* art. 17, p. 656.

7. Champlin, *op. cit.,* p. 14.

8. Carol Luebering, *To Comfort All Who Mourn* (Kansas City, Mo.: Celebration Books, 1980), p. 13.

9. Troy Organ, "Grief and the Art of Consolation: A Personal Testimony," Chicago: *The Christian Century* (August 1-8, 1979), pp. 759-762.

10. The Family Life Education Office of the diocese of Syracuse has produced a well-received practical manual, *Hope for Bereaved.* It contains a wealth of material for both the bereaved and those who minister to the grieving. For example, the section headed "Experiences of Grief" diagrams these attitudes, feelings, and acts of the grief process and explains them in detail. (Copies are available at $6.50 each or $6.00 each for orders of ten or more copies from Family Life Education, c/o Hope for Bereaved, 1342 Lancaster Ave., Syracuse, NY 13210.)

11. Organ, *op. cit.,* p. 762.

12. Joseph Bayly, *The Last Thing We Talk About* (Elgin, Ill.: David C. Cook Publishing Co., 1973), p. 66.

13. *Ibid.,* pp. 55-56.

14. *Ibid.,* p. 55.

15. Organ, *op. cit.,* p. 762.

16. "Business Bulletin: Medicine — A Special Report," New York: *Wall Street Journal* (September 20, 1984).

17. Organ, *op. cit.,* p. 762.

18. *Ibid.*

19. Judith Tate, *Learning to Live Again: The Journey Through Grief for the Widowed or Divorced* (Cincinnati: St. Anthony Messenger Press, 1979), pp. 121-122.

20. *Ibid.,* p. 122.

21. *Ibid.*, pp. 25-28.
22. Paula Ripple, F.S.P.A., *The Pain and the Possibility* (Notre Dame, Ind.: Ave Maria Press, 1978).
23. *Ibid.*, pp. 46-47.

Chapter 12

1. Raymond A. Moody, Jr., *Life After Life* (New York: Bantam Books, 1975), p. 16.
2. *Ibid.*, pp. 58-73.
3. *Ibid.*, p. 79.
4. *Ibid.*, p. 81.
5. *Ibid.*, p. 84.
6. Andrew Greeley, *Death and Beyond* (Chicago: The Thomas More Press, 1976). Peter J. Kreeft, *Heaven: The Heart's Deepest Longing* (San Francisco: Harper and Row, 1980). Peter J. Kreeft, *Everything You Ever Wanted to Know About Heaven* (San Francisco: Harper and Row, 1982). David E. Rosage, *Living Here and Hereafter* (Locust Valley, N.Y.: Living Flame Press, 1982).
7. Kushner, *op. cit.* [see ch. 5, note 1, above], pp. 28-29.
8. William Kirk Kilpatrick, New York: *America*, bk. rev. sect. (March 26, 1983), p. 247.
9. Enrico Garzilli, "For to Those Who Love God," published by F.T.T.W.L., Box 3672, Rolfe St., Cranston Branch, Providence, RI 02910.
10. MacNutt, *Healing, op.cit.* [see ch. 9, note 2, above], pp. 248-261.
11. MacNutt, *The Power to Heal, op. cit.* [see ch. 9, note 24, above], p. 155.
12. Sheldon Vanauken, *A Severe Mercy* (New York: Bantam Books, 1977), pp. 159-160, 175-176.